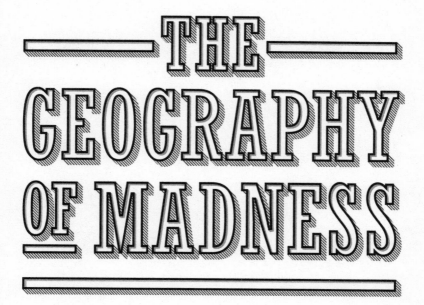

THE GEOGRAPHY OF MADNESS

FRANK BURES

THE
GEOGRAPHY
OF MADNESS

PENIS THIEVES
VOODOO DEATH

AND THE SEARCH FOR
THE MEANING OF THE WORLD'S
STRANGEST SYNDROMES

MELVILLE HOUSE
BROOKLYN • LONDON

THE GEOGRAPHY OF MADNESS

Melville House Publishing   8 Blackstock Mews
46 John Street   and   Islington
Brooklyn, NY 11201   London N4 2BT

mhpbooks.com   facebook.com/mhpbooks   @melvillehouse

ISBN: 978-1-61219-372-4

Design by Christopher King

Printed in the United States of America
10 9 8 7 6 5 4 3 2 1

A catalog record for this book is available from
the Library of Congress

For Bridgit, for everything

Heaven have mercy on us all—Presbyterians and Pagans alike—for we are all somehow dreadfully cracked about the head, and sadly need mending.

—HERMAN MELVILLE, *Moby-Dick*

CONTENTS

INTRODUCTION

In 1990, I left a small town in the Midwest and went to Italy to spend a year as an exchange student. What I encountered there was a shock, and what followed was one of the most difficult years of my life. When I got home, I was not the same.

How was that possible? How could moving from one place, from one language, from one culture to another . . . change who you are? Yet it did. After one short year immersed in Italian society, I felt like a different person, and I was disturbed by the depth of this change. I didn't feel completely American any more, but neither did I feel Italian. I had, it seemed, left something behind.

What I didn't know at the time was that that year abroad marked the beginning of a quest—one that would take years to understand, let alone complete. *The Geography of Madness* is the story of that search, which would take me to places I'd never dreamed I'd go—to Nigeria, Thailand, Borneo, Singapore, Hong Kong, China, and elsewhere. In those places I found wandering fox ghosts and lizards that crawl under your skin, poison pork, and poisoned minds. I also came to see how our ideas can kill us, how our beliefs can save us, and how these things quietly determine the course of our lives.

They can also cause your penis to disappear. That was what I found when I went to Nigeria to investigate the phenomenon of "magical penis theft," where people felt that their genitals had disappeared—that they'd been stolen away through sorcery. Magical penis theft was known in the medical literature as *koro*, and was considered a "culture-bound syndrome." The victim feels his (or occasionally her) genitals being sucked into his (or her) body. If this transpires, death will ensue.

But even as I found myself fascinated by the cases of these thefts, another question grew in my mind: What would it feel like to live in a world where such a thing were possible—where at any minute your penis could be whisked away? This question would lead me, in turn, to the deeper questions underlying it. Namely: What is culture? What is it made of? And how are we bound to it?

For much of the twentieth century, this question was fiercely debated, but in the 1990s—the era of globalization—it was abandoned by serious thinkers. Instead, they argued that culture could not be defined because it was everything that we do. Meanwhile, others pointed out that if culture was everything, then it was also nothing. In the end, the word came to seem like a hopeless paradox, and the world simply moved on.

But I couldn't move on. I knew that culture wasn't nothing. I knew this because I had looked into the eyes of Starrys Obazi, whose penis had been stolen on a street corner in Lagos. I knew it because I had felt culture's power myself, and had been trying to understand it ever since.

Now, after years of asking questions, after traveling through these places, I believe I have the answers I sought, not only about what culture is, but also about how it makes us sick and well, sane and insane; how it gives us hope and takes it away; how it tells us who we are and who we are not; how it shapes us and how we shape it.

Much of what you'll encounter in the pages that follow will seem impossible, or at least hard to believe, but this is a work of nonfiction. All conversations and events here took place, and are reproduced as faithfully as possible. Some grammar has been corrected for reading purposes, but this was checked with the speakers whenever they could be reached. More to the point, the worlds I've tried to convey here do exist and are real to the people in them. As you read on, and as we travel together, I hope they will become more so to you as well, and that the lines between the real and the imagined, between the familiar and the foreign, begin to blur. By then, I hope you'll come to see the part we all play in creating worlds that look strange from outside but that make perfect sense from within, and how the strands that hold those worlds together are the same threads that run through our lives, and that hold us together too.

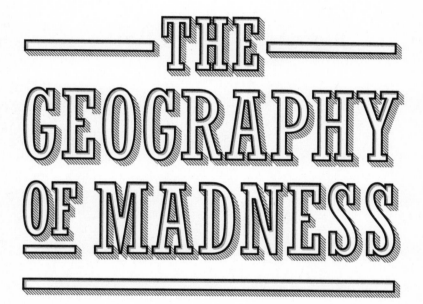

1

THE CASE OF
THE MISSING MANHOOD

The sun was high and the day was already hot when our car rolled into Alagbado, a dusty, run-down town on the far edge of Lagos, the Nigerian mega-city where a young man named Wasiu Karimu was reported to live.[1] His penis had been stolen.

A few days earlier, his name had appeared in the paper: The headline read: "COURT REMANDS MAN OVER FALSE ALARM ON GENITAL ORGAN DISAPPEARANCE." It said that a certain Wasiu Karimu was on a bus when he "was said to have let out a strident cry, claiming that his genital organ had disappeared. He immediately grabbed [Funmi] Bello, who was seated next to him, and shouted that the woman should restore his 'stolen' organ."

The two of them got off the bus, and a crowd of "miscreants" swarmed around Bello, ready to kill her. But a passing police patrol intervened, stopped them from lynching her, and escorted the two to the police station. There Karimu told the commissioner "his organ was returning gradually."

The paper gave the address where Wasiu Karimu lived, so I decided to try to find out what exactly had transpired in his pants. A friend named Toni Kan had lent me his car, and had asked Akeem, his mechanic and sometimes driver, to take me out to the place.

We drove past clapboard shacks and little restaurants, through huge muddy pools, past people watching us from doorways, until we came to the address in the paper. Chickens and goats scattered in front of our car, which said PRESS on the windshield. (Toni freelanced for a few Lagos papers and magazines.)

Wasiu Karimu's house was an ample, two-story affair with a little shop next to it. We got out and asked a girl working inside if he lived there.

"Yes," she said, "but he is not around."

Akeem went into the yard of the house, and a woman jumped in front of him. She said she was Wasiu's mother and began yelling at Akeem to get out of the yard. He retreated to the car, and for a few minutes, we stood in the middle of the road, in the sun, waiting for Wasiu Karimu to show up. But after about twenty minutes, several young men came around the corner and took up posts around the house. A couple of them were holding long sticks.

Akeem turned to me. "Local Area Boys," he said.

In Lagos, the Area Boys were thugs—a law unto themselves. They had multiplied after the military dictatorship fell in 1998, seeding a new kind of terror throughout the city. These boys had an ugly swagger. I could see sweat start to drip down Akeem's head. He turned to me.

"Let us go," he said.

"Wait a minute," I said. We'd come a long way—in fact, I had come all the way from America just for this, and this could be my only chance to talk to someone whose penis had actually been stolen. So I made us wait. I figured we weren't doing any harm—I just wanted to ask a few questions. I walked over to the shop next to Wasiu Karimu's house and bought a bottle of coke.

"Sir," said the young girl at the shop as she handed me the bottle, "Are you looking for someone?"

"Yes," I said. "Wasiu Karimu."

"Sir," she said, "maybe you should just go now, before there are problems. It will be easier for everyone."

I quickly finished my soda and walked back to the car.

"Okay," I said to Akeem. I was beginning to feel sick, and now my own back was drenched with sweat. "Let's go."

Akeem shook his head and looked down the road. It had been cut off with two large wooden blocks and a car. There was no way out.

One of the Area Boys who was guarding Wasiu Karimu's house looked particularly eager to deliver some punishment. He ran into the street with his cane and whacked it on the ground. "We will beat the press," he yelled. "We will beat the press."

The young men huddled together in front of the house. After a long delay, they called Akeem over. He talked to them for a little bit. Then they called me over. They wanted to see the article about Wasiu. I pulled the wrinkled photocopy out of my pocket and handed it to them.

A quiet man in a 50 Cent T-shirt was clearly the leader. He took the article, unfolded it, and read through it.

"Let us see your ID," he said. I hadn't brought my passport, for exactly this reason, and my driver's license had disappeared from my hotel room. All I had with me was an expired YMCA membership card, which I handed over.

The leader, whose name was Ade, took it. He handed it to a lanky man with crooked teeth, who looked at it briefly, then handed it back.

"Do you know who we are?" asked Ade.

I did not.

"We are OPC. You know OPC?"

The OPC was the O'odua People's Congress, a quasi-political organization that was halfway between the Area Boys and a militia. They were violent and arbitrary. Recently, they had killed several policemen in Lagos, and in some parts of the city they were being hunted by the government.

"We have to make sure," Ade said, "you are not coming here to do some harm. Maybe you were sent here by that woman." The woman, he meant, who stole Wasiu Karimu's penis.

There was a crash, as a glass bottle exploded against one of the tires on our car. Both Akeem and I jumped.

"No," I said trying to be calm. "I just want to ask some questions. Is he around?"

"He is not around."

He was. Unbeknownst to me at the time, Wasiu Karimu himself was apparently listening from a distance. Akeem told me later he was sure he had seen him—a little guy standing at the back, young and nervous.

The men talked among themselves in Yoruba, then Ade's henchman with the bad teeth told the story. Wasiu, Bad Teeth said, had gotten on the bus and sat down next to this woman. He didn't have a watch, so he asked her what time it was. She didn't know. Then the conductor came around and asked her for her fare. She didn't have that either. As she stood up to get out of the bus, she bumped into Wasiu.

"Then," he said, "Wasiu Karimu felt something happen in his body. Something not right. And he checked and his thing was gone."

"Was it gone," I asked, "or was it shrinking?"

"Shrinking! Shrinking! It was getting smaller."

And as he felt his penis shrink, Wasiu Karimu screamed

and demanded the woman put his penis back. The conductor told them both to get off the bus, and a crowd closed in on the accused, not doubting for an instant that the woman could do such a thing. But as soon as she saw trouble coming, Bad Teeth said, she replaced Wasiu's manhood, so when the police took him down to the station, they thought he was lying and arrested him instead.

"What did she want the penis for?" I asked Bad Teeth.

"For juju," he said, "or maybe to make some money."

Behind us, from the corner of my eye, I could see that the roadblocks had been removed.

"Do you have anything else you want to ask?"

"No," I said. "I don't think so."

"Okay," he said. "You are free to go."

"Thank you."

I nodded to Akeem. We got in the car and drove away.

For several years before I came to Nigeria, I had been following reports of cases like Wasiu Karimu's in the region. It all started in 2001, when I came across an article on the BBC's website that read 'MISSING' PENIS SPARKS MOB LYNCHING.[2]

In that incident, at least twelve people had been killed by an angry crowd in southwestern Nigeria after being accused of "making people's genital organs disappear." Eight of the accused were members of an evangelical brotherhood. They'd been attacked by angry locals and burnt alive.

The article referred to a similar incident the previous month in a nearby Nigerian state in which six people were killed. The police, according to the latest report, claimed to have things under control, after deploying plainclothes detectives "to keep an eye on those they accuse of raising false alarms."

The images kept playing in my mind. Yet I struggled to imagine the fear and panic that would erupt in such a raging lynch mob. Whether or not penises were really disappearing, it was clear people believed that they were—so strongly that they were willing to kill for it. Was this just fear? Was it belief? Wasn't it an easy thing to check? Or was there more to it than that? I'd lived in East Africa for some time, where I learned that stories came in layers. Just when you thought you'd gotten to the bottom of one, you peeled it back and another appeared. Perhaps Nigeria was like that too.

A few months later, I saw another BBC report: BENIN ALERT OVER 'PENIS THEFT' PANIC.[3] In that country, which borders Nigeria to the west, more people had been killed by mobs who accused them of magical genital theft. A photojournalist and a high school principal had made narrow escapes. In total, five people had died in at least ten attacks. Four were burned to death. One was hacked to pieces.

Penis theft, in other words, was serious business. Yet there was something about the dismissive tone of the latter article that bothered me. Especially this sentence: "The belief that men's private parts can mysteriously disappear through a handshake or an incantation is commonplace in Benin where superstition and illiteracy are rife."

This felt empty to me. It had the ring of history, of superiority. The article seemed to suggest—or to claim—that civilized people were free from superstition, that education was the cure for penis theft, and that literacy could make us less crazy.

For reasons I didn't quite understand at the time, I wasn't as ready to dismiss these incidents as primitive naïveté. That felt too easy. I was sure there was more at work, and I couldn't help wanting to explore not just Nigeria, but any place where such things were possible—where magical penis theft made perfect, terrifying sense. Something made it feel real. Something stitched that world together. Was it the same thing that had once stitched mine together? And was it the same thing that had pulled it apart? I knew that someday I would have to go there to find out.

I printed out the second article and put it in my file. At the time, I was living in Portland, Oregon, working at a large bookstore, and freelancing for some local papers. I wrote a pitch for a story about magical penis theft and sent it out to several men's magazines—the logical audience.

One by one the responses came. The story was too expensive. It was too risky. It was too weird. I had a phone conversation with an editor who liked the idea, but said he couldn't pay for me to fly to Nigeria to find essentially . . . nothing.

I didn't have a good response. After all, I didn't really know what I would find, or even what I was looking for, and no one was going to send me there to figure that out. Yet while I couldn't quite articulate the story I wanted to tell, I knew it wasn't about nothing. Rather, it seemed to me like a story about everything—not just penis theft. I put the articles back in my file, and tried to put the story in the back of my mind.

Meanwhile, life went on. My wife Bridgit and I left Portland to spend a year in Thailand, then moved to Madison, Wisconsin. We bought a house and soon learned we would be having a daughter. But amid all the excitement, I felt a stab of panic. Nigeria gnawed at me. I knew that it was a terrible time to leave. I knew that Bridgit, newly pregnant, wouldn't want me to go.

But I also knew that I had to, and that if I didn't it would be a lifelong regret. Before we entered this new chapter of our lives, I had to close this last one. Because if I waited until after our daughter was born, I might never make it to Nigeria. And if I didn't, I feared I might never find this thing I was looking for.

So I started scraping money together. And I started trying to navigate Nigeria's mystifying visa process: For several weeks I called the Nigerian Embassy in Washington, but no one ever answered. Finally I called the Nigerian Consulate in New York. I called and called. I made complex calculations about the best time to catch someone in the office (around 10 a.m., I believed) until I finally did. The man I talked to explained the process, which was arcane and baffling and designed to discourage tourists: You really had to want to go there.

Three months later, I was the lone tourist on a plane full of Nigerians descending into Lagos. They were dressed in designer jeans. Their bags were bursting with gifts. When we landed, the cabin door opened and I smelled cooking fires and diesel fumes mingling in the thick, tropical air.

The Murtala Muhammed International Airport was shabby from years of neglect. The floors were battered and chipped, and the place felt oddly desolate, like a Detroit bus station. Nonetheless, I found my bags, shouldered them, and headed out into the city of 17 million souls.

In my pocket I had one name: Toni Kan, a friend of a writer I knew.[4] Toni and I had e-mailed a bit, and he had said he would meet me at the airport. Clutching my bags, I went outside and scanned the mob of shouting taxi drivers, but I didn't know what he looked like, and no one seemed to be looking for me. So I waded into the drivers and bargained hard. After some ruthless back-and-forth I got one driver down to around $30 (which I'm sure was too high). I got into his car and we drove off toward the only hotel I could find that cost less than $300 a night: The Mainland Hotel, a sagging, decrepit building across the Carter Bridge from Lagos Island, the heart of the city.

In the hotel, ceiling tiles in the hall were broken and stained and hanging down in places. A musty smell drifted up from the carpet. When I shut my room's door behind me, I found that the lock was broken. So I called downstairs, and soon two men from maintenance arrived. After an hour of tinkering, the lock seemed to function well enough. I thanked them, and lay on my bed to watch the news: The cameras showed a series of beatings by unruly crowds somewhere across the city. These had something to do with kidnappers who were stealing people and using their body parts for witchcraft.

Everyone, it seemed, was afraid, and it was with images of angry mobs and missing penises running through my mind that I finally faded into sleep.

The next morning, I woke up to a sound I couldn't place—a din, a low roar. It seemed to be coming from my window. I got up, opened it, and realized that this was just the sound of the city: The clamor of the millions of people of Lagos, arguing, yelling, laughing. It was louder than any metropolis I'd ever been in. Closing my window again didn't make much difference. I walked downstairs, but I steeled myself near the front door for a few minutes before heading out. Then I walked out the door and into the streets.

To call Lagos "vibrant" is a vast understatement. It is something much more than that, with an energy like I'd never felt before. I let it carry me along. I walked like I knew where I was going, even though I had no idea. I walked over the bridge to Lagos Island. I walked through the streets, which were packed with people. I didn't know where to begin looking for penis thieves. I stopped in bookstores. I took motorcycle taxis. I asked people I met for help, but without much luck or any insight.

Eventually I found my way to Jankara Market, a collection of cramped stands under a patchwork of corrugated-iron sheets that protected the merchandise from the rain and sun. Spread out beneath them were branches, leaves, seeds, shells, skins, bones, skulls, and dead lizards and toads, all of which are said to contain properties that heal, help, or harm, depending on what you need them to do.

The market was also known for the darker things you could buy there. Specifically, juju: magic. On my first visit to Jankara, I met a woman named Edy. She was short and well fed. We talked for a while before she announced that she loved me and wanted to marry me. When I told her I was already married, she threatened to bind me to her with magic, using two wooden figures, so that I would not sleep at night until I saw her.

A few days later, I came back and found Edy's stall. As soon as I walked into the dark, covered grounds of the market, she saw me.

"Ah," she said. "You have come back!"

"Yes," I said.

"Sit here," she said, and pointed to a bench. She sat down across from me. "What did you bring me?"

I showed her some fruit I had brought.

"Ah, very nice," she said and started to eat, even though it was daytime in the middle of Ramadan and she was Muslim. "How is your wife?"

"She is good."

"And what about your other wife?"

"Who is that?"

"'Who is that?'" she said in mock surprise. "I think you know who that is. That is me."

"That is nice," I said. "But in America it's not possible."

A man came up to her and handed her a crumpled piece of paper with a list of ingredients on it. She peered at the list, then got up and went around collecting sticks and leaves and seeds and small branches. She chopped them all up and put them in a bag. While she was doing this, the man sat next to me on a bench.

"Is that for you?" I asked.

"Yes," he said. "It makes you very strong."

Then another man came up and put in his order. It was something for the appendix, he said. When he was gone, Edy again sat down across from me.

"I have a question," I said.

"Yes."

"In my country, we don't have juju."

"Yes."

"But I was reading in the paper about penis snatchers—"

"Ah," she interrupted me. "Don't listen to them. That is not true. If I touch your thing like this"—and here she touched my leg—"is your penis gone?"

"No," I said, uneasily. "But what if I come to you and ask you for protection? Can you do it?"

"Yes, I can."

"How much?"

"One thousand naira. Two thousand. Even up from there." This was a large sum by Nigerian standards—more than $15.

"Do you have many people come and ask for this?"

"Yes," she said in a low voice.

She looked around.

"Many."

• • •

The first recorded incident of penis theft in Africa I could find took place in Sudan in the 1960s.[5] But in the mid- to late seventies in Nigeria, there were waves of well-documented cases. One of these happened in the northern city of Kaduna, where a psychiatrist named Dr. Sunday Ilechukwu was working in his office when a policeman arrived, escorting two men.[6] One of them said he needed a medical assessment: He had accused the other of making his penis disappear.

As with Wasiu Karimu and the crowd outside the bus, this had caused a disturbance in the street. During Ilechukwu's examination, he later recounted, the victim stared straight ahead while the doctor examined his penis and pronounced him normal.

"Exclaiming," Ilechukwu wrote in the *Transcultural Psychiatric Review*, "the patient looked down at his groin for the first time, suggesting that the genitals had just reappeared."

According to Ilechukwu, this was part of an epidemic of magical penis theft that swept through Nigeria between 1975 and 1977. "Men could be seen in the streets of Lagos holding on to their genitalia either openly or discreetly with their hand in their pockets," Ilechukwu wrote. "Women were also seen holding on to their breasts directly or discreetly, by crossing the hands across the chest . . . Vigilance and anticipatory aggression were thought to be good prophylaxes. This led to further breakdown of law and order." During an incident, the victim would yell: "*Thief! My genitals are gone!*" Immediately, a culprit would be identified, apprehended by a crowd, and often killed.[7]

Then, for some reason, the panics died down. Around 1990, though, there was another resurgence, and sporadic outbreaks continued for the next decade and a half at a steady clip. Then came the attacks I read about in Nigeria and Benin.

One survey counted fifty-six separate incidents of "genital shrinking, disappearance, and snatching" across West Africa between 1997 and 2003, in which at least thirty-six suspected penis thieves were killed at the hands of mobs.[8] These cases were often reported only in local newspapers, remaining little known outside the region.

The world, for its part, greeted news of these thefts with a mix of disbelief, dismissal, and amusement, some of which were evident in that BBC article about Benin. Did these people really believe this? Couldn't they just check? These were not unfair questions, but the tone in which they were asked harked back to another era, not so distant from our own, when this behavior would have been classified as superstition, or "primitive reactions," or "ethnic psychosis" by Western doctors. The implication would have been clear: These were the imaginary products of simpler minds.

One day, after walking around Lagos fishing for stories of penis theft, I decided to take a taxi home, rather than walk. Traffic was jammed, and it took us what felt like hours to get off Lagos Island. Finally, the driver inched onto the Carter Bridge, and we crawled across the water to the other side. Ahead of us, I could see the Mainland Hotel rising above the low, corrugated iron roofs. We were almost there when the taxi stopped.

In front of the car stood a group of policemen. Some of them had machine guns. A few of them were policemen in uniform. Most did not. The ones that didn't were Area Boys, working with the police. One of them approached our car. He was a big man with a deadly-cold look on his ruddy face, which filled my window as he stuck his head into the car. He looked at me. He looked at the driver. He looked back at me.

"Where were you walking?" he asked.

"What do you mean?" I asked.

"I saw you walking here, this way." He pointed down the street from where we'd come.

"Just around."

"Where's your passport?"

"I don't have it," I lied.

"Don't have it? Okay. Out of the car."

I got out of the car. People were staring. A crowd started to form. The other "police" watched with interest.

"What's in your bag?" he asked.

I lied again. "Nothing," I said. In the bag were all my papers, some books, and $200 I'd just changed to naira. The money was right on top, and I knew from years of travel in places like this that to show it to him would be the worst possible tell in the poker game we were playing, which I couldn't afford to lose—I was already running low on cash. There was no way I was going to open my bag.

"Let me see."

"No," I said. "Look, I can just walk back to my hotel." I pointed down the road. Then I started walking. He stepped in front of me. Then he lifted up his shirt and pulled a gun out of his belt.

"Get in the car," he said.

He went back to talk with the other Area Boys. While he was gone I reached in and shoved the money to the very bottom of the bag. Just then a uniformed policeman in a bulletproof vest came over.

"What's in your bag?"

"Nothing," I opened it and showed him. "Just books. Papers."

The policeman left, and I could see the Area Boy coming

back. The taxi driver turned to me and whispered urgently, "Just give him some little money!"

I pulled out 500 naira, equivalent to about $4.

"No! No! Not five hundred!" the driver said. "Just two hundred."

I put the N500 back and the driver quickly handed me N200. The Area Boy stuck his head back through my window.

"Let me see in your bag."

This time I showed him the papers and books.

"Why didn't you show me before?"

"I was just nervous," I said,

I handed him the N200. He took it, and looked around furtively. Then he slid it into his pocket, as if no one knew what he was doing. He stepped back from the car and waved us on.

We pulled away and the driver turned to me.

"Now give me that five hundred!"

If Lagos was a city with unparalleled energy, I could see how quickly the tide could turn against you. There was a palpable sense of vulnerability, of forces that were beyond your control. Every time you went out the door, you had to have your wits—and more—about you.

Back at my hotel, I lay on my bed, still shaking a little. I thought about calling home, but Bridgit burst into tears every time I did, and I was sure she didn't want to hear about this. So I watched the news on TV instead: a police station had been burned down by the army, after a policeman slapped an army officer at a checkpoint; a young boy had been accused of being a kidnapper, was caught by a crowd, and burned alive.

The TV didn't prove much of a distraction from the Area

Boys, so I pulled out a folder with some reading material. I had printed out a few articles at the medical library in Madison about magical penis theft. Cross-cultural psychiatrists referred to it as "genital retraction syndrome," or *koro*, a name that originally came from Asia. At the time, *koro* was usually included with a grab-bag of other exotic mental conditions not found in the West. These were referred to as "culture-bound syndromes" (or, more recently, "cultural syndromes"), mental illnesses that could only arise in certain cultures.

Koro was not the only culture-bound syndrome found in Africa. There were others as well, like *ode ori*, in which certain people in the Yoruba part of Nigeria felt an organism crawling through their head, causing dizziness and vision loss. There was *brain fag*, in which students experienced painful neck and eye symptoms, as well as cognitive disruption, after prolonged studying. There was *mamhepo*, in which a victim mimics a particular animal chosen by a witch—a condition said to be caused by selfishness. And there was *voodoo death*, or "psychogenic death," in which a person was cursed, informed he or she would die at a given time, and then did.

Like penis theft, all of these syndromes were terribly real to the people who experienced them. But why was it that they existed in some places and not others? Did where you lived determine how you lost your mind? Would a person who goes mad in one culture go mad differently in another? Or, maybe, would she not go mad at all? What, come to think of it, was a "culture," anyway? And how tightly were any of us bound to it?

After a few days, Toni Kan and I finally managed to meet up, and he was kind enough to let me stay at his place—a huge step up from the moldering Mainland. Toni was a fiction writer and a journalist, and he had many friends who worked in Lagos's media. One day, we met with several of them at an outdoor restaurant across the road from the National Theater, where we discussed the literary scene in the city, which was undergoing a renaissance. We sat talking and drinking for several hours. The journalists were funny and sharp and opinionated—they were curious, well read, and interesting. They were intellectuals.

After a while, I brought up the question of magical penis theft, and asked if anyone had heard of it. Did that really happen? An editor named Jossy looked me in the eye.

"No," he said. "It doesn't happen. I'm telling you, it is purely a myth."

More drinks arrived. More opinions were offered. And I observed how over the next hour or so, the center of gravity shifted. One writer mentioned an inexplicable incident that had involved his aunt. Magic, he implied, had been involved. Another editor offered up a similar story about something that had happened to a sister. Toni added a story about a girl in his apartment building who'd been given what she thought was water by a stranger. When she woke up, she found she had taken a bus across the country, and she was missing the money she was supposed to put in the bank—the water had had *juju* in it. Jossy then told me about a witchdoctor who could locate any item that had been stolen. We talked about the "kidnappers" roaming the streets looking for people whose body parts they could use for rituals. (One of the newspapers had run articles of "10 ways to prevent kidnapping" and "8 tactics employed by kidnappers.")

To doubt one of these stories was to doubt the person sitting next to you. But to doubt *all* the stories felt like something else, like lifting a much heavier weight. With each anecdote, I could feel stitches beings sewn, as if I were being drawn closer to a place where such things seemed possible. It was a visceral shift—in my stomach, rather than my head. These guys didn't seem crazy or gullible. Aren't there, I found myself asking, things in this world we just don't understand?

Near the end, Jossy looked me in the eye again. "It is true," he said. "Penis snatching—it happens. No question. And there is someone I know who it happened to."

It took a few days to track him down, but eventually we found Starrys Obazi. By that time, Akeem and I had been out to Wasiu Karimu's house. And as close as that was, I still needed to hear from someone who'd felt the theft, who had been at the scene of the crime, and who could say exactly what it was like. This was my best hope. So we arranged to meet at a cheap fast-food place on the north side of Lagos.

Starrys was already waiting when Toni and I arrived. He was a wiry little man with a nasal voice. Together, we ordered our food, and sat down at a table by the window. Around us, other Nigerians walked past with their trays and sat down to eat their burgers, watching hip-hop videos on the television behind us. Starrys dug into his chicken like the hungry, unemployed journalist he was.

For fourteen years he'd been an editor at *FAME*, a Nigerian celebrity tabloid, until the publisher mysteriously stopped paying him. Jobs, even low-paying editorial jobs, were rare in Lagos, and it had been several years since Starrys had had one.

The theft of his penis, he explained, had occurred in 1990, while he was still a reporter at the *Evening Times*. At that point, he was a skeptic himself—and a Jehovah's Witness. He knew about penis snatching. He had heard the stories.

Maybe he had even written them. But for his part, he wasn't really concerned about such things.

Then one day, when he was waiting for a bus on his way to work, a man approached him and held out a piece of paper with a street name on it.

"Do you know where this is?" the man asked, without saying the name. Starrys didn't know the street. For some reason, he didn't believe that the street really existed. Something felt strange. Then another man appeared behind Starrys and explained where the street was—without seeing the paper. This was even stranger. Together, the two men walked away, and Starrys started to feel something he had never felt before.

"At that moment," he said, leaning forward, "I felt something depart my body. I began to feel empty inside. I put my hand into my pants and touched my thing. It was unusually small—smaller than the normal size. And the scrotum was flat. I put my fingers into the sockets, and they were not there. The testes were gone. And I was just feeling empty!" His voice strained as he recalled the panic of that day.

Starrys ran after the men and confronted them. "Something happened to my penis!" he told the stranger who had asked for directions. The man said he had no idea what Starrys was talking about. Something told him not to shout, he said. "Because as soon as I shouted, he would have been lynched. And if he was lynched, how could I get my penis back?"

Starrys finished eating his chicken and wiped his hands. "It was one quarter of its normal size," he said. He voice strained with emphasis, as if, even now, he couldn't quite believe it had happened. But he did believe it. And as I listened to him tell his story, I felt myself drawn into it. I could feel his fear. I gave in to the panic in his voice. It was so real, so true. In that moment, I was afraid, too.

He continued with his story. Despite the men's denials, one of them agreed to accompany him to a nearby hospital to document the theft. But just as they arrived at the hospital, the man grabbed Starrys and shouted, "LET'S GO *IIIIN!*" and something happened.

"When he grabbed me," Starrys said, "I felt calm again. I felt an inner calm. I checked my testes, and they were there." He checked his penis as well, and the missing three-quarters had returned. The doctor examined Starrys and pronounced him fine, though he also warned the stranger to quit causing trouble on the street.

I was getting close—I could feel it. Listening to the stories of friends of friends; reading the newspaper reports; feeling the fear and hatred of the OPC; sitting across from Starrys and hearing the panic in his voice. These had brought me near the place I'd come looking for: to the very edge of belief itself, to a world of magic. There I could feel a hint of fear. Since I arrived, Lagos had changed. It had begun to feel dangerous, and its dangers plausible. The stories I'd been told had shifted something deep down. They had carried me down a different stream. And before I left, I had to see if I could drift a little farther.

And so, on one of my last days in Lagos, I headed out into the streets. The winding roads were packed with people. Tens of thousands coming and going, moving along sidewalks, jamming the streets so thickly that cars had to push through them at a crawl, blaring their horns and parting crowds like the earth before a plow.

I was far from Jankara Market when I started walking, and I didn't know where I was going. My only wish was to see if I could brush up against the boundary that separated my world from this other, more elusive one. I wanted to cross over—not just to be hearing the story, but to become part of it. I wanted to look back and see someone checking if his manhood was in place.

I moved with the crowd. We were packed together, but rarely touched. Streams of people ran easily alongside each other. I went deeper into the city, watched people pass within inches of me, then feint and slide by, barely brushing me. I tried to nudge a few people with my shoulder, but most were too fast, too alert, too leery.

Walking along, I caught one man on the shoulder with mine. But when I looked back, it seemed like he hadn't even noticed. I clipped another man a little harder, but it was like I wasn't even there. I bumped a few more people lightly, until finally I caught one man hard enough that I'm sure he knew it was purposeful.

I stopped to look at him. But he didn't reach down and grab himself. He didn't point to me. He didn't accuse me. He didn't even look back. He just moved on. And it was then that I realized I could drift on this river, but never sink into it. It flowed around me, but not through me. I was in the water, but not of it.

When I'd landed in Lagos, I didn't know it, but this was what I had been looking for. Whether actual penis theft was real hardly mattered, because the currents that carried it through the culture—the stories—were real to those who told them, heard them, and lived them. I could feel this in a way I hadn't before. But I also knew I would have to go farther to unravel this knot of culture and strangeness, to understand how it worked, and where its power came from. I didn't yet know how I'd do it, but I knew I'd have to follow the river to the source.

2

FOLLOWING THREADS

Back home, I typed up my notes, and as I read through them, what struck me was not how strange everything seemed, but how mundane. When I looked up and found myself in Wisconsin, it seemed odd that there were no Area Boys, or lynch mobs, or magic flowing through the streets. The roads were paved. The police and army were not at war. The electricity was constant, infinite.

Yet whenever I told my American friends about Nigeria, it was impossible to describe what I'd found there without it sounding hollow and unreal. It was impossible to explain the feeling of being there—the *normalcy* of it, the sense it made.

This was not the first time I had felt this kind of loss for words. Over the years, I'd often felt that my experiences in other cultures surpassed my ability to describe them. The first time this happened was during one of the hardest years of my life, when I had left the Minnesota town where I grew up and set out into the world.

Our town was called Winona, and it was ringed by bluffs that ran along the Mississippi River.[9] We knew about the world out there, but our horizon was a close one, and what went on beyond the hills didn't seem to have much to do with us.

Then one year when I was in high school, we were visited by an exchange student from Italy. She had long dark hair and a beautiful smile. Her name was Anna, and she was staying with some friends of my parents. After a few months, they informed us that Anna's younger brother also wanted to come to America and was looking for a host family. My parents put the question to me: Did I want to go to Italy?

I didn't know what to say. I didn't *not* want to go to Italy. I was in no hurry to go to college. Something like this had simply never occurred to me. And since I didn't have any other plans, I said yes, not knowing how drastically the course of my life had just changed.

The following summer, Anna's brother Fritz arrived. He fit in well with our family of three boys, but not so much into the larger society of Winona. This was in 1989, and globalization hadn't really made its way to the upper Midwest, so Fritz's European styles stuck out in our working-class town: The high water jeans, the wingtip shoes, the funny haircut. These all marked him for social death—or relegation to the foreign exchange students' lunch table, which amounted to the same thing.

One night, my friends and I were going to a party and we took Fritz along. It was a kegger being thrown by some guys who'd graduated a few years earlier, but who'd never quite moved on. When we arrived, one of these types stood at the front door making sure no nerds got in. He eyed me warily, then let me pass.

But once I got inside, I could hear arguing behind me. I walked back to the door, where the bouncer was pointing to Fritz's pants and telling him he couldn't come in. "But why?" Fritz asked, looking down at his jeans.

"What's the problem?" I asked.

"This guy's wearing jeans," he said.

The rest of us were in shorts. Wearing jeans in summer was definitely not cool.

"It's okay," I said. "He just got here. He's from Italy." I rolled my eyes to show how clueless Italians were about style. He narrowed his eyes, looked Fritz over, then waved us through.

Over the next year, Fritz's English got better, and we became friends. After I graduated, he went back to Bologna, the city where he lived, and I soon followed. There were eight children at his house, which was set high on a hill outside the city. On school days, the five oldest kids and I would pile into the family car, race into town, and climb out in front of our school.

I was placed into the "scientific" stream because it was closer to the American curriculum than the "classical" or the "linguistic" ones. But only Italian was spoken, and the Spanish I'd studied for years wasn't much help. I sat next to my deskmate, Filippo, for weeks, then months, not understanding a word. I'd jot down random vocabulary and occasionally some profanity, which Filippo supplied me with. Then, at one o'clock, we would pile back in the car and drive up the hill for the family meal.

Fritz's family had moved to Italy from Germany when he was very young, and both languages were spoken in the house, which was run with a mix of German rigor and Italian passion. Our days were rigid, and all the formality—the greetings, the attire, the rules—soon began to grate on my nerves. I couldn't see any point to it. One day, I was sitting at the table, happily shoving pasta into my mouth and gulping down whole glasses of water, when Anna spoke up.

"You know," she said, "you'll never get a girlfriend if you keep eating like that."

"Eating like what?" I asked.

"Eating like this," she said, and did her best impression

of a prehistoric man feeding off a mammoth leg. I got a little defensive.

"What does it matter," I snapped, "as long as the food gets into your mouth?"

"That is *so* American," she said. "Here it is not like that. For example, Constanza is thinking about breaking up with her boyfriend because his manners are so bad."

"Really?" I asked.

If she'd wanted to get my attention, she had it: Constanza was her beautiful, dark-haired friend, on whom I happened to have a terrible crush.

As my frustrations grew, I felt like Fritz back home in Minnesota, staring down at his jeans and asking, "But why?" Mine were acid-washed, but now they just looked old and strange. So many things I'd assumed were true and solid no longer seemed so. All the ways I knew of being funny or cool or stylish or smart were gone. Every day I broke an endless list of rules that I had no idea existed, rules I didn't understand or believe in. When I reached my foot out for certainties, nothing was there. The scripts I'd learned back home—which I'd never given any thought to, because they were all I knew—had been torn up. I'd been handed new ones that I couldn't read or understand.

Fritz would try to explain these things to me, but much of it was beyond explanation. So I would lay on my bed and stare at the ceiling, trying to remember how I had been back home. Outwardly I got through the days, but inside it felt like something had broken, like I had no idea who I was supposed to be.

At Christmas I went back to Winona for two weeks. When I got there, everything was strange, as if I'd landed on the moon. Time seemed to move in slow motion. The words people said, the jokes they told, sounded like they were coming through a tiny speaker. And I wasn't the only one who felt confused: one friend remarked at how odd I was acting.

When people asked me about Italy, I couldn't quite figure out how to explain it. I couldn't find the words. There were too many invisible things. That was when I realized I had started to understand that place in a new way, and now couldn't quite bridge the distance back home. I'd changed: I wasn't the same person who'd left this place. My connections to my home had been severed—and while I could certainly mend them (even after a few days back, I began to feel better), it was clear that in a short time I'd left one culture behind and started to become part of another.

After New Year's, I went back to Bologna, and things finally started to click. My language accelerated. Filippo and I became close friends. At dinner, I drank my water more slowly and ate according to the new ways. Most surprisingly, I did all this happily. It suddenly made sense, even though only a month earlier, it hadn't. New ways of thinking, of acting, of being were unrolled before me. The scripts that had seemed so confounding started to make a kind of sense, their wisdom growing clearer all the time.

When I got home, I didn't know where I belonged. Part of me wanted to be back in Italy, where I had learned so much and had more to learn; part of me wanted to go elsewhere, because there were so many other places to explore; part of me wanted to sit and study to try to understand the world and the experiences I'd had, moving from one culture to another.

College wasn't much help on that front. At the time, multiculturalism was the dominant creed, according to which cultures were fragile things that had to be protected and preserved, like delicate statues to be placed around campus so as to maximize our "diversity." Cultures could barely be discussed and never criticized, only revered—despite the fact that none of us really knew what they were. All we knew was that they made us different.

I paid lip service to this idea, but I could never whip up much enthusiasm for it. Even then, having felt the strange power of immersion, of what used to be called "culture shock," I knew there was more to it. I knew that culture shaped not only how the world looked, but how it felt, and how we find our place in it. I knew that culture was powerful and tangible—I just didn't yet know much else.

How I could move forward through all this wasn't at all clear until a man named Paul Gruchow came to speak to my English class. Gruchow was a well-regarded nature writer who lived near our school.[10] He was bald and portly, with a quick laugh and a look in his eye like his mind was always partly elsewhere. His beard made him look like a professor, which he sometimes was.

I don't remember much of what he talked about, but I do remember being somewhat starstruck. I'd started to think that writing might be my best path among those I could see, but I had no idea where to begin. Now, in front of us was a writer, living proof that such a thing was possible. Could I do that? And how did it even work? What did I need to do?

I wanted to know the secrets to the world Gruchow inhabited, so after class, I got in touch with him, and he invited me to his house a few days later.

Patiently, he told me about his life, about his work at a small newspaper, about his first book, and his many struggles along the way. When I asked him for advice, he waved me off. He warned me that this path was full of hardship and disappointment and that there were seven times as many people who wanted to be writers as could be.

"Don't do it," he said, "unless there's nothing else you can do."

We sat for a long while, and I listened as he talked, hearing mostly the parts that I needed to hear. This, I see now, was what I was looking for: A story on which I could model my own.

Just because you know where you want to go, however, doesn't mean you know how to get there. Now that I had a goal in mind, a dream, I had to figure out the steps that would take me to it. College was coming to a close, and I had to do something, go somewhere: either go to school or go out into the world. Bridgit and I had been dating since our first month of college. We were still very much in love, but I wasn't ready to settle down. I wanted the opposite. I wanted to be unsettled. The thought of sitting in another classroom was unbearable. I started asking other writers for advice, for clues. One told me I needed to fill up with things to write about. Another said to me that if I wanted to teach, I should get a degree. But if I wanted to write, I shouldn't. And so, to the world it was.

By chance, a professor I knew was leaving academia to run a teaching program in Tanzania, where she had deep roots (she and her husband had been among the first wave of Peace Corps there). She was looking for people to teach for a year at the private schools she would be working with. Bridgit had other plans, so we agreed to spend the year apart. We both knew it was for the best, but amid the tears, I was afraid I'd chosen a path I would regret—that I was choosing ambition over love.

Nonetheless, I flew to East Africa, and in the northern

city of Arusha, I moved into an old colonial house at the end of a dirt road. It was being refurbished to be a teaching center, and I was to be its first resident in many years.

For several weeks the house had no water, so I took a bucket to a nearby stream. The house was a short walk from my school. In my room upstairs, I had a desk and a bed and a small propane stove. At night, I would write in my notebooks by the light of a bulb that hung over my desk. When the electricity failed, I used candles. I wrote about teaching, about school, about money, about religion. I wrote about beer and littering and avocados and many, many other things.[11]

The days became weeks, then months, and once again I started to feel deep changes. As I got to know my students and neighbors, and how they viewed the world, my life there took on a different texture. Time expanded around events, rather than contracting to constrain them. The flow of days was more measured, less frenetic. We foreigners were called *wazungu*, which came from the Swahili verb *kuzunguka*, meaning "to run around in a circle," and I could see that this was true. I began understand the deeper meaning of words like *kusindikiza*, or "to accompany someone part of the way home," as locals walked with me for miles along the road. I began to understand the proverb *wageni ni baraka*, which means "guests are a blessing," when peoples invited me to sit with them for tea or a meal. I saw that this new world was filled with gestures that showed how people enjoyed your company and how they valued your presence more than your absence. These realizations awakened something in me that I didn't even know was there. I tried to capture it in my journal, but I didn't know how to write about such things yet. Still, they filled me up.

After a year, I returned home. For some months, Bridgit

and I reconnected, then packed our things into a U-Haul and headed west to Portland, Oregon. There, after some time, I found a job at Powell's Books, surrounded by the very things that I wanted to do, and to be.

When no one was watching, I would stop in the Africa section. It was huge, and filled with many bad books, but also some good ones. I would run the process backward, try to figure out how each book came into being, how these things were supposed to go. Other times, I would stand in the used-magazine section and do the same, paging through old issues of *Granta*, which had some of the stories and writers I loved best: Bill Bryson, Bruce Chatwin, Martha Gellhorn, Ryszard Kapuscinski.

Soon I started sending out some pieces I'd written about Tanzania. Eventually, a few got published. At the same time, I started writing for local publications, and I began to get a sense for the shapes of stories. I didn't yet understand how they worked, but soon enough, I could feel my way through them.

I kept writing, kept working. Bridgit and I got married, and though life seemed to be moving into another phase, it seemed like we still had time for another adventure, one more year abroad, this time together. After a long search, we got an offer to teach English at a school in the far south of Thailand, which was barely part of Thailand at all.[12]

This time, I had a concrete plan. I would write a book with an arc, a story about our year of stumbles and learning and ultimately getting to know our students and ourselves. It would be about bridging gulfs, about crossing divides. I was picturing, this time, a kind of Thai version of Peter Hessler's *River Town*, about his two years teaching English in China.

Within a few days of our arrival, however, it was clear the story I hoped for was not the one that was going to unfold here. Our school was located in the town of Yala, near the Malaysian border, in an area that had been disputed for one hundred years. Most local people weren't ethnically Thai, nor were they Buddhist, but instead were Malay and Muslim. Many, including Bridgit's kindergarteners, didn't speak a word of Thai, only the local language, Malayu.

Also, a separatist war was brewing. Yala's policemen were being shot. Motorcycle bombs were going off around town. Osama bin Laden's image was stenciled on car doors and printed on T-shirts sold in the market. In a nearby town, a school was burned to the ground.

After a few weeks, Bridgit began to despair. She hadn't really wanted to teach in the first place, and our situation seemed grim. Besides, Yala was a depressing place, with nothing do except eat dinner at the lone hotel, where a bar girl sang sad songs to an empty room.[13]

The only other foreigner in town was an enormous American named Greg. He would take a weekly bus ride to a nearby city with his Philipino wife, where they would purchase a several days supply of Kentucky Fried Chicken.

One night, I came home and found Bridgit packing her bag, ready to leave under the cover of darkness. But I talked her down, and we were able to make a more graceful exit. Before the end of our second month, we were on a train to Bangkok.

Riding north, I watched through the window as my hopes receded; my notebook filled with just a few pages of a story that would never be written.

Far to the north, in the megacity, we found an apartment on the twentieth floor of a building next to a canal. From the window, we could see Bangkok, City of Angels, spreading out to the sea.

Now that we weren't teaching, it wasn't clear exactly what we were doing. But we had committed to being in the country for a year—that was the plan—and decided to stick to it. We had some savings, and if I could make some money freelancing, it would work. So I bought an old laptop from the back room of a computer mall and immediately set about writing pitches, which I sent from an internet café a few blocks away.

This went well at first. I got a handful of small assignments from national magazines back home. One was for a story about a physicist studying how fish swim. Another was for a piece about medical tourism. Another was about the tensions building in the south.

But slowly, as I tried to put them together, these stories fell apart. The fish wasn't photogenic enough. The looming Iraq War meant that almost no Americans were traveling abroad for medical tourism. And the south had become too dangerous for me to visit.

Then, I received a life-changing e-mail. It was from the editor of *Granta*, who wanted to assign a story I'd pitched about Bruno Manser, a Swiss idealist and activist (and shepherd), who'd disappeared on the island of Borneo. Manser had traveled to Borneo in the mid-1980s, where he was adopted by a tribe of nomadic forest dwellers called the Penan. He learned their language and for six years, he roamed the jungle with them.

Soon, however, logging started to encroach on their territory. Malaysia was selling massive amounts of timber to Japan and Korea, and the Penans' home was being consumed. Throughout the 1990s, Manser helped them organize protests and road blocks. As a result, he became a target of the Malaysian government, with a rumored bounty on his head. Then, in the year 2000, he crossed the mountains that ran along the border with Indonesia, and came down to a village called Bario. From there, he set out into the woods and was never heard from again.

In early 2003, I flew to Borneo. I found people who'd known Manser. I talked to some of the Penan. I interviewed Manser's brother, his girlfriend, his friends. I traced his route to the last place he'd been, near Bario, which at that time was still unreachable by road. Then I flew back to Bangkok, and poured everything I had into the story. Finally I felt I'd arrived; finally I felt like I was doing what I should be doing; finally I felt like the course I plotted had wound around to the point I'd been aiming for. My hard work had paid off. My writing career had truly begun. Soon my work would sit alongside that of the writers I loved.

When I sent in the story, it topped 12,000 words. I waited for a response, and I waited some more. It came: The story was rejected out of hand. I wrote and begged for a chance to revise, to rewrite, but never heard back. I sent in a revision anyway, but all I got in return was a check for part of my expenses. And so, dead broke and unsure if I knew how to write any kind of story, I helped Bridgit pack our bags for home.[14]

We settled in Madison, Wisconsin, which was far quieter than Bangkok. It felt like we were far away from the world. It felt like a retreat. The sense of defeat hung over me. I wrote for the city magazine and some local papers[15] and found a job doing data entry at a bookstore. Occasionally I would apply for other jobs around town and not get them.

Every few months, I would return to the Bruno Manser story. I would sift through it obsessively, trying to figure out where I had gone wrong, not only with Manser's story, but also with my own. When I reread it, I could see it was dead on the page, and I knew the editor was right to kill it. But I couldn't figure out why. I rewrote it over and over, trying to bring it back to life. Ultimately, I came to see that I had included so much detail that it was impossible to tell why any of it mattered. I had written an exhaustive account, a chronology. What I had not written was a story. I wrote what had happened, but not why.

At the bookstore, there was a partial wall between my desk and the restroom. I put on headphones to drown out the sound of our customers relieving themselves. Occasionally, the owner would stick his head in the room to tell me something I'd done wrong. Otherwise I was alone, and I sat wondering—baffled at how I'd ended up there, so far from where I thought I'd be. How does anyone know the right way to turn, the right choice to make, the right risk to take? What do you do when the life you imagined seems so far from the one you are living?

Then, one day while I was sitting at work, I got an e-mail from a friend who edited a literary travel writing website called World Hum, which had run a few of my Tanzania essays. He said he had good news to tell me on the phone.

Puzzled, I called him, and he announced that one of my essays had been picked for the *Best American Travel Writing*. It would run alongside some of the very writers I used to read while hiding in the stacks at Powell's.

This wasn't the story I'd imagined for myself. But maybe it was one I could work with. For the first time in months, I felt hopeful. Maybe I could do this thing after all. Maybe I could be a writer.

And before long, I was dreaming of Nigeria.

3

CULTURE BOUND

After I got back from Nigeria, I worked on the story about it for months. I spent hours in the medical library, paging through old journals, reading case studies, and trying to make sense of the so-called culture-bound syndromes listed in the back of the Diagnostic and Statistical Manual, the bible of modern psychiatry.

In addition to *koro*, there were many mental illnesses that the average American wouldn't recognize. Some were simply unimaginable. There was *amok*, from Malaysia, in which a person brooded for a period of time, then went on a random homicidal rampage, but had no memory of the events afterward.[16] Also in Malaysia, certain people were said to suffer from *latah*, where a sudden fright puts them in a trance, during which they were compelled to imitate the words and actions of those around them.[17] (This mainly tended to affect middle-aged women.)

In Japan, certain people suffered from *taijin kyofusho*, a terrifying fear of other people's embarrassment (not their own). This had several subtypes: "*sekimen-kyofu* (the fear of blushing), *shubo-kyofu* (the fear of a deformed body), *jikoshisen-kyofu* (the fear of eye-to-eye contact), and *jikoshu-kyofu* (the fear of one's own foul body odor)."[18] Young Japanese also were diagnosed with *hikikomori*, an extreme social withdrawal that had become something of a "silent epidemic" in Japan.[19] Sufferers refused to leave their rooms for years, and were sometimes treated for necrosis in places where their skin began to rot. This condition seemed to be related to the Japanese belief that we all have inward and outward selves—and to a concern about the masks behind which we hide. Often the afflicted are unable to draw their mothers' faces.[20]

In Cambodia, people suffered from *khyâl cap*, or "wind attacks," in which *khyâl*, a "wind-like substance" believed to flow alongside blood, rushes to the head and causes all kinds of problems, including dizziness, shortness of breath, numbness, fever, and so on. *Khyâl* attacks could be caused by "worry, standing up, a change in the weather and any kind of fright, such as being startled or awakening from a nightmare." It was said to cause asphyxia, bursting of the neck vessels, and cardiac arrest.[21]

Indian men were at risk of *dhat syndrome*,[22] in which they lost weight and felt fatigue, weakness, and impotence due to loss of semen—one of seven essential bodily fluids in Ayurvedic medicine. In some parts of the country, they also contracted *koro*: In 1982, eighty-three men and women in Lower Assam rushed to hospitals with a "tingling" in their lower abdomen and a fear that their testicles or breasts were shrinking.[23] In nearby North Bengal, there were 405 such cases.[24] And in the Bikaner district of Rajasthan, patients who suffered from *gilhari syndrome* arrived at the hospital with swelling on the back of their neck, complaining that a gilhari (a kind of lizard) was crawling under their skin, terrified that they would die if it reached their neck.[25]

The research was mesmerizing. I had, by this point, seen just how powerfully culture could shape our perception and behavior, but was this deeper than just perception? There were so many strange fears, so many different ideas of how the human body intersected with the world. These syndromes hinted at beliefs that were impossibly foreign to me, worlds even stranger than the one that had produced magical penis theft. What would it be like to have a lizard crawling under your skin, or to feel wind flowing through you, or to always wonder who was hiding behind the masks of everyone you knew?

How can we understand these things? How could we know what they might be like to experience? They come from stories we don't know told in languages we don't speak. They emerge from a history of which we are not part, and from worlds we do not agree exist. In China, for example, people could be stricken with *frigophobia*, or the "morbid fear of cold (*pa-zeng*), fear of loss of vitality, excessive fear of the wind (*pa-feng*), and the need to wear excessive clothing."[26]

This was a fear rooted in the belief that life was a balancing act between yin and yang—between cold and hot, light and dark—and imbalances create illness. In that world, there are five phases, five states of matter—wood, fire, earth, metal and water—and each of these are correlated with a color, a taste, a smell, a human sound, an emotion, a virtue, and two organs—one for yin, one for yang.[27]

To me, reading about these ailments on paper was one thing. But I knew that it would take years to really know them. One had to be among them, to understand them from within, and ideally to speak the language, because most of these syndromes didn't even have useful equivalents in English. Any attempt to translate them had to involve some distortion. Ted Kaptchuk, a Harvard researcher who studied Chinese medicine in Macau, wrote that it took him years to see that "Chinese medicine contained wheels within wheels and that the traditional one that I had studied was far from the whole art of healing."

Yet to the people who lived in these places—who grew up there—all of this made intuitive sense. Something like *frigophobia*, utterly foreign to us on the outside, could be both logical and visceral to those on the inside.

As I read more about culture-bound syndromes, it became clear that you didn't have to travel all the way to China to encounter such strangeness. Europe, I learned, had had its share of genital theft issues. That may have been why magical penis theft seemed easier to grasp than worrying about one's "earth organs." In 1487, two German clergymen published the *Malleus Maleficarum*, the guidebook to witches and their ways, warned that a witch could cause one's *membrum virile* to vanish, and several chapters were dedicated to the topic.[28] Likewise, the *Compendium Maleficarum* noted that witches had many ways to affect one's potency, the seventh of which included "a retraction, hiding or actual removal of the male genitals." (This could be either a temporary or a permanent condition.)[29] Even into the 1960s, there were reports of Italian migrant workers in Switzerland panicking over a loss of virility caused by witchcraft.[30]

But the cultural changes that Europe had undergone during the Renaissance and the Enlightenment, along with the rise of science, empiricism, and a more mechanistic view of the world, had diminished the power of such ideas.

Chinese medicine, on the other hand, remained consistent. It was never overtaken by religion (as European medicine had), and can still trace its roots back to the *Nei Ching*, the Yellow Emperor's *Classic Text of Internal Medicine*, which was compiled between 400 and 100 BC. It was in that book that the mortal dangers of *suo yang*, or "shrinking penis," were first sketched with a warning that "illness due to cold causes retraction of the penis . . . Death usually occurs in Autumn."[31]

This warning echoed through the centuries. Around 200 AD, a physician named Zhang Zhongjing (known as the Chinese Hippocrates) mentioned *suo yang* in his *Treatise on Febrile Diseases Caused by Cold* and described the symptoms as: "the penis twisting upon itself . . . and on the sixth or seventh day, there is shrinkage of the scrotum and coldness of the extremities . . . the sufferer will not be able to drink, he becomes unconscious."[32]

Around 600 AD, another physician, Sun Simiao, noted that excessive sexual intercourse could result in "injury to the qi" or the energy of life (also spelled "ch'i"), in which "the tongue becomes contracted, the lips become pale, the testes shrink, abdominal cramps occur . . . an intense feeling of impending doom follows."[33]

In an 1835 collection of medical remedies, Pao Siaw-Ow described *suo yang* as a "yin type of fever"[34] (meaning that it arises from too much cold) and recommended that the patient be treated with some hot yang for balance.

By the time the first Westerners started to get wind of this, in the late 1800s, Europe's witch hunting days were long past, and most people had forgotten to be worried about their *membrum virile*. So they were surprised to find this fear among the people they were colonizing. The first European to make a note of it was a Dutch colonist named Benjamin Matthes, who lived on the island of Sulawesi, in what is now Indonesia. In 1874 Matthes was compiling a dictionary of Buginese when he came across the term *lasa koro*, which meant "shrinking of the penis," a disease that Matthes said was not uncommon among the locals and "must be very dangerous."[35]

It was a fear that had been sown throughout the region, and which was strong well into the twentieth century, which saw large-scale epidemics in the 1960s, 1970s, and 1980s in Singapore, Thailand, India, and elsewhere.[36] The biggest took place in southern China, on the Island of Hainan. It began in the fall of 1984 and went on through the following spring, passing through small villages. By the end, a fox spirit believed to be wandering the island, stealing men's genitals while they lay in their beds at night, had attacked several thousand victims.[37]

For Western doctors, these things were little more than curiosities. In 1942, *Stitt's Diagnosis, Prevention and Treatment of Tropical Diseases* classified several such conditions under the heading "Diseases of rare occurrence or of doubtful origin."[38]

Unlike our own illnesses, which were purely biological, these were dismissed as the products of weak, primitive minds. According to Laurence Kirmayer, editor of the journal *Transcultural Psychiatry*, it was believed that "southern or non-Western peoples had underdeveloped frontal lobes and hence were prone to disinhibited behaviors," meaning they weren't evolved enough to have real mental illnesses.[39]

But in 1948, a young man arrived in Hong Kong who would change all that. Pow Meng Yap grew up in Malaysia and studied Psychological Medicine at Cambridge.[40] After that, he came to Hong Kong to take over the Victoria Mental Hospital, which he began to reform immediately. Under him, Victoria would become a laboratory of modern ideas and techniques.

Not long after he arrived, Yap noticed a number of patients with a curious affliction. These were young men concerned that their penises were being sucked into their bodies, and who were convinced that if this happened, they would die. The incidents usually occurred at night, after masturbation or intercourse or a cold bath. Most of Yap's patients recovered with a combination of psychotherapy and drugs, although a few still suffered occasional bouts of anxiety. One patient did not improve at all, but fortunately, none of them actually died.

Yap had been thinking about the intersection of culture and mental health for some time—he was fascinated by the way psychiatry was influenced by culture, and vice versa. In France, he wrote, neurologists could induce a hysterical attack by pressing on a patient's "hysterogenic points," while doctors across the channel in England couldn't seem to locate them.[41]

What we consider pathological, Yap pointed out, depends on what we consider normal. And European and American ideas of normal were "neither necessarily the commonest nor the most healthy,"[42] and they certainly couldn't be exported wholesale to the rest of the world. "In psychiatry we tread on uncertain ground," he wrote. "Even within one culture . . . ideas of what constitutes abnormality may vary," and we should avoid, "thinking that psychological normality is a special attribute of Western civilization."[43]

Culture, Yap thought, influenced the kinds of mental problems seen in a given society, and in 1965, he published a paper in the *British Journal of Psychiatry* titled, "*Koro*—A Culture-bound Depersonalization Syndrome," in which he argued that "culture-bound syndromes" depended on patients "learning a certain cluster of beliefs,"[44] which shaped the form of the illness as well as its occurrence.

For the Chinese, a belief in the possibility of *koro* was therefore not abnormal. It had deep roots and grew out of a system of beliefs that went back thousands of years. And this, in effect, was part of the cause.

Which part was not yet clear. But for the first time, a phenomenon like *koro* started being taken more seriously by Western psychiatry. As Yap pointed out, just because they weren't our syndromes, didn't mean they weren't real.

• • •

Almost three years after I returned from Nigeria—and seven years after I first learned about magical penis theft—my story about investigating the phenomenon in Nigeria appeared in the pages of *Harper's Magazine*. When it came out, I did a few interviews, and heard that one teacher even got fired for assigning the story to his class. I felt bad about that, but I also felt relieved that it was finally out in the world.

And yet there were parts of it that bothered me, loose ends I hadn't been able to tie up, questions I had raised, but not answered.

These centered around the idea of culture, about what it was and how it worked. They were huge, old, and difficult questions, and while it would have been foolish to try to deal with them too much in a magazine story, I felt I needed to keep digging. I felt like there was something else I needed to know.

I continued to read the literature on cultural syndromes, and after a while, I noticed that the word "narrative" kept coming up. In the late 1970s, an anthropologist named Arthur Kleinman began to make an argument not unlike Yap's: mental illnesses were shaped by the cultures in which they appeared,[45] and we couldn't simply export our mental categories wholesale. Yet where Yap saw culture as a larger organism we were all part of, Kleinman saw that a person's own story of his or her illness played a role, as well.[46] A psychiatrist had to understand how patients viewed themselves and their illnesses, and what forces they felt were at the root of their suffering.

The power of narratives, of stories, was certainly something I had felt in Nigeria, in Italy, in Tanzania . . . everywhere. By then, Bridgit and I had two daughters, and as they grew, I began to see a similar power at work in their lives. Around the time our oldest turned four, she started making what seemed like odd requests. "Tell me about the sad parts of your life," she would say at the dinner table. Or, "Tell me about the scary parts of your life."

This phase went on for a while. I played along, telling her about my appendectomy in Africa, about the time I almost fell off a cliff, about the fishhook that went through my finger. We talked about deaths in the family, and she would sit with her eyes wide, not saying a word, listening as if her life depended on it.

It wasn't until I'd gone through a whole list of broken bones and broken hearts that I realized what she was really asking: How can I deal with sadness? What should happen when I'm afraid? She was looking for scenarios out of which to build her own, for clues about which way to turn when she reached those crossroads herself. The stories, for her, were like maps to the world.

After that, I started paying closer attention to the books we were reading them, to the movies they watched, and to the stories we shared. These, I came to see, were doing some work deep within them, providing them with outlines and scripts that would help them get through whatever might unfold in their lives, with the choices they would eventually have to make. The stories they heard were paving the roads in front of them. They were shaping the world as they entered it.

Time went on. I felt I was getting closer to the answers. I was building a bridge from Italy to Nigeria and beyond. I knew I would still have to go farther. In one paper, Yap had quoted the Swiss physician Paracelsus, who said: "The doctor must be a traveler because he must enquire of the world."

The next time a window opened, I knew I had to go.

4

MODERN MINDS

Over the years, I developed an ease at moving in and out of different cultures—learning languages, adapting to different ways of thinking. And while this would seem like an advantage for a travel writer, I find the opposite to be the case.

Whenever I land in a new place, my mind goes back to the words of the English philosopher Herbert Spencer, who wrote about a Frenchman who, after three weeks in England announced he wanted to write a book about the country. After living there for three months, he decided he still wasn't ready. And after three years, he concluded that he knew nothing about England at all.[47]

Immersion is about going below the surface, about realizing how much you don't know—at least at first. So when I landed in Hong Kong, I knew that the Cantonese phrase book in my pocket would only get me so far. Language, after all, isn't the only doorway to a people's secrets and stories—just the first one. Nonetheless, I had a sense that I would find something here, the same feeling that had drawn me to Nigeria.

I got off the bus in Wan Chai, the old red light district, and found the hostel I'd booked. The door was almost invisible from the street, and when I got off the elevator, I could see it was incredibly cramped. People sat at their computers, knees almost touching, headphones in, not speaking a word.

The only person who talked to me was a surly kickboxer from Montenegro who'd come to Hong Kong to try to start a business selling champagne and watches. This was going badly, he said, since he discovered there already were plenty of watches and even more champagne in Hong Kong.

The next day I set out across Hong Kong Island, a dense forest of skyscrapers. The first place I wanted to go was the old Victoria Mental Hospital, where Yap arrived in 1948,[48] fresh from Cambridge with his new ideas about drugs and electroshocks and lobotomies, which he began performing there.[49] On my way, I stopped at a place I'd seen on the map, a lovely, two-story brick building called the Hong Kong Museum of Medical Sciences.

The museum had a warm, old-world feel. There were hardwood floors, molded plaster ceilings, and a grand staircase that led to the second story. There was even a fireplace.

The building had been the Bacteriological Institute, erected in 1906 to help fight the epidemic of Bubonic plague in the surrounding neighborhood. After a massive outbreak in the nearby city of Guangzhou that killed some 80,000 people,[50] the disease soon spread to Hong Kong, where bodies began piling up. At night, the dead were dumped into the streets and the harbor.

No one knew what had caused the plague. The Chinese believed it rose up from the earth when the ground was dry and porous. The English believed it was caused by "the filthy habits of life amongst the 210,000 Chinese who reside here."[51]

The British colonial government struggled to get the disease under control. After 7,000 Chinese were evicted from their homes, rumors began to spread that English doctors would slit the bellies of pregnant Chinese women, then scoop out babies' eyeballs to make plague medicine. At one point, two foreign women doctors were attacked by a mob.[52]

By 1905, however, scientists had figured out the culprit—fleas—and outbreaks were slowly brought under control.[53] The victory over the plague turned out to be a turning point in local attitudes toward Western medicine—people in Hong Kong began to see how powerful it could be. Given that history, I assumed that the Museum of Medical Sciences would be a sort of shrine to Western medicine. But that wasn't the case at all. In fact, the first thing I saw was a sign that said, THE MEDICAL CLASSIC OF THE YELLOW EMPEROR, next to a 1910 copy of the founding text of traditional Chinese medicine, which contained some of the earliest references to the perils of *suo yang*.

Throughout the museum, two worlds—and two sciences—were on display side by side. One exhibit discussed the role of ephedrine in both Chinese and Western medicines. In another room, there were posters that featured Western descriptions of an organ's function on one side, and the Chinese on the other: In the West, the spleen cleans the blood and can cause harm when it gets enlarged. In China, the spleen was one of five "Zang organs" that stored qi, and problems with it could be seen in "luster manifesting on lips, in secretions such as saliva and as thoughts in the mind."

I'd read about the basic tenets of traditional Chinese medicine—and thought I understood them, at least superficially. Yap had written that "the Chinese traditionally viewed the universe as a vast organism of which Man was just one part."[54] The body was believed to be a microcosm of the larger world.

And yet, confronted with this belief in person, I was mystified. It simply didn't seem believable, didn't feel remotely plausible. In his book *The Healing Arts*, Ted Kaptchuk writes: "Medicine is the application of what people think is true about the cosmos to what is experienced in everyday life."[55]

But while this had been easy to accept in a book, only now did I get a sense of the distance between this world and my own, between the two sciences. Like everyone in my culture, I grew up believing the body was a machine, that sickness came from broken parts, and that doctors were like mechanics. I couldn't see any connection between my liver and my thoughts.

Downstairs in the front hallway, I was greeted by an older Chinese woman who spoke in a crisp British accent. She had a grandmotherly manner, and was dressed like she was on her way to church. She was a retired pathologist named Dr. Faith Ho, who volunteered at the Museum. I asked if she had ever heard of Pow Meng Yap.

"Oh yes. I remember him!" she said. "When I was a medical student, he taught us at the old High Street Mental Hospital. And he'd just opened the new Castle Peak Hospital, but he still had patients here."

"What do you remember about him?" I asked.

"He was very gentle. He was quiet. As students, we certainly didn't know much about his research. But he died in the 1970s, right?"

"Right," I said. "In 1971. That was the year I was born."

I looked back at the museum. I asked her what people in Hong Kong thought about the two medicines.

"Well," she said, "I think almost everybody in Hong Kong would attend to both Western and Chinese traditional medicine. The layman would think Chinese medicine is good for some things and Western medicine is good for others."

"Is the belief in traditional Chinese medicine going down?"

"No!" she said. "It's resurgent. People are very interested in it—it's stronger now than before." Dr. Ho looked at her watch and realized she was late for a meeting and excused herself, but handed me her card.

I followed her outside and then continued to wander away from the city center, until I came to the old Mental Hospital, which, when it was first built, had been called the European Lunatic Asylum.

From the street, the building, with its long row of arches, seemed to bear the weight of history. Yap had worked here for thirty years. It was here that those young men had come, holding on to their penises, terrified that they were near the edge of death.

I tried to go inside, but to my surprise, the actual building was gone. It had been torn down, and something new built in its place. The old stone arches had been preserved and bolted to the new structure behind it. All that was left was the façade.

The next day I left the hostel, made my way to the metro, and caught a train out to Castle Peak, the place Dr. Ho had mentioned. It was here that Yap had built his new hospital so many years ago.

The train sped across the New Territories—once Hong Kong's rural, agricultural countryside. Now towering apartment blocks lined the way.

Nearly an hour from the city center, the train stopped and I got out. To the west, I could see the craggy outline of Castle Peak, a low mountain on the edge of Shenzhen Bay. Back when Yap had first come here, the landscape was rich with fish farms and fruit trees—a peaceful repose for troubled minds.

I knew the general direction and started walking that way—uphill, on back roads, behind houses, past apartments and factories—until I came to a high fence that enclosed the Castle Peak Hospital. The campus was enormous. The buildings were white and new—the original structures had been knocked down in a renovation a few years earlier.

I followed the perimeter to the entrance, where a confused security guard took my name. I told him I was here to see the library, if there was such a thing, and in a few minutes, a friendly young woman named Natalie came out to greet me. She worked in the public relations department, and led me through locked doors and gated areas, until we came to the Hospital Museum, which felt like a kind of shrine to Dr. Yap. There was a faded photo of him sitting at his desk and another one of him with his wife and two children, with the simple caption, "His family." In each photo his hair was neatly combed; his thick-framed glasses sat above his reserved smile.

On a small table I found a huge green book with embossed gold letters that said: "Collection of Publications by Professor Yap Pow-Meng." It began with a list of nearly fifty academic publications, starting in 1944, when he was still studying in England, and ending in 1977, six years after he died.

Yap's range of research was stunning. There was his paper on "possession syndrome," comparing French and Chinese sufferers who believed themselves to be taken over by spirits. There was a study of the high rates of alcoholism in Hong Kong's Europeans compared to low rates among the Chinese. There was a fifty-page paper on "The Latah Reaction" from Yap's native Malaysia (*latah* was already in decline when his paper was published in 1952).[56]

It seemed clear that his thinking was decades ahead of its time and ran far beyond the borders of Hong Kong. He wrote about history and philosophy. He wrote about the existential tendencies of European psychiatrists and the mechanistic ones of the Americans and British. He noted the way every culture has its own "mental health ideology" which derived from its religious principles. (America's mental hygiene movement, he argued, was closely linked to Boston's puritan physicians).

He observed how the Western mental health ideology failed in China, "partly because eastern bottles have not been emptied of the old wine, and partly because the new has not been found to agree with the palate."[57]

I shut the book and looked out the window. Behind the hospital, Castle Peak rose up to the sky. It made more sense now, having seen Hong Kong myself, that Yap had come to these realizations here, where cultures mingled for centuries. Yap himself had been raised in one culture, educated in another and worked in another still.

It was no wonder that he had such a clear view of how our culture shapes the contours of our mind.

A few days later, I was walking through Hong Kong's Central District looking for an address. When I came to it, I ran down the listings until I arrived at the name: Dr. Wai Hoi Lo, another of the few people alive who had known and worked with Yap. It had been twenty years since Dr. Wai himself had retired from the government health services, but at eighty-two, he kept up his own practice and was going strong.

The building was occupied by doctors practicing both Western and Chinese medicine. I took the elevator up to Dr. Wai's floor, then walked down the long, wood-paneled hall to his office, where he sat hunched in his chair. He had white eyebrows and black hair and wore thin-rimmed glasses. He asked me to sit down. I was worried he might not be able to hear my questions, but he caught what I said, including everything I asked about Dr. Yap.

"Of course, I remember him well!" he said. "Dr. Yap was always so busy."

"And do you remember at all what he was like?" I asked.

"He was very quiet. He was interested only in reading, especially things to do with psychiatry. And he was very knowledgeable about what was going on in the world of psychiatry. But he was solitary, and we were under him, so we didn't really go in and talk to him. He was kind, to me at least, and his English was very good. But his Chinese needed a lot of help from his wife. He was most interested in the cultural aspects of psychiatry."

"Like *koro*?" I asked.

"Yes. I remember in 1967, when Yap was president of the Hong Kong Psychiatric Association and I was the secretary. At that time, we had an epidemic of *koro* in Hong Kong. Not very large one—only a few cases a day for a week or so.[58] Most of them were low education, illiterate. They heard about it over the news, then became scared. But it became contagious, so we wrote an article to all the Chinese newspapers and requested they not publish cases of *koro*. Of course, not all of them listened to us. But after this, the *koro* cases were diminishing."

"And do you see any cases these days?"

"A lot of people know what *koro* means. But now, Hong Kong is really quite Westernized. Nowadays, the sort of cases I see here are no different from what I saw in the UK in London. I haven't seen *koro* for a long time. I think all these cultural syndromes will decrease, when people have higher education."[59]

That evening I went down to the harbor. After dark, the "Symphony of Lights" show began. Laser beams flashed from the skyscrapers, set to music that came from speakers around the city. The lights danced on the water, beautiful and surreal. But all I could think about was everything that remained under the surface.

5

SAVAGE MINDS

Was Dr. Wai right? Was education all it took to rid the world of culture-bound syndromes? And was that happening now? Were *koro* and *latah* and everything else I'd read about on the cusp of being educated off the face of the earth? Would we end up with nothing but pure chemistry?

This was the implication of much of the discussion of culture-bound syndromes: That they were the product of ignorance;[60] that they were not real. With education, they would go away.

Many people held this view, particularly in the West. But it didn't quite seem right to pit education against culture—to make them opposites. After all, we certainly had culture in the West. The idea seemed to be that education would eliminate wrong beliefs, and leave nothing but biology behind. But this was pitting culture against biology, which didn't seem right either. As Yap had noted, while there was certainly biology at work, culture had its own power as well, and that power wasn't just limited to non-Westerners. But what *was* it, exactly? How did it work? This was something that, for all my research, I hadn't quite pieced together for myself. I had started with the dictionary, but most definitions simply called it, "the total pattern of human behavior and its products," or something along those lines. This was the same as saying,

"It's what we think and do," which begs the question of where those patterns came from, how they change, and how they change us. If certain syndromes are culture-bound, what are they bound to?

I couldn't find the answers to these questions anywhere. The more I looked into it, the more I began to understand why. "Culture," the social historian Raymond Williams once noted, "is one of the two or three most complicated words in the English language."[61]

The earliest meaning I could find traced back to the Latin word *cultura*, meaning the cultivation or tending of a growing things, such as crops or animals. That was what the word meant in most European languages. But around the sixteenth century, English writers and philosophers like Thomas Hobbes, Francis Bacon, and Thomas More began using it in discussions of the mind, which they believed was something that also needed proper cultivation to grow.

Then, in the 1800s, when German philosophers were building their theories of human evolution, trying to explain how we had gone from the state of nature to the nation-state, they seized on the word "culture" and equated it with "civilization." Gustav Klemm proposed that humans pass through three stages of evolution: savagery, domestication and freedom.[62] Baron de Montesquieu called these *savagery, barbarism* and *civilization*.[63] After that, Culture and Civilization began to blur into the same thing.

The English ethnologist E. B. Tylor was a man who kept up on such things. He was well-versed in German philosophy, and like his continental counterparts, he believed in the upward trajectory of human evolution. Tylor was born in 1832 into a London family that owned a brass foundry. He started working there when he was sixteen, but by the time he turned twenty-three, he had begun to develop signs of "consump-tion" (most likely tuberculosis), and his doctor advised him to travel to the tropics.[64]

In 1856, Tylor sailed for Cuba where, on an omnibus in Havana, he happened to meet a banker and ethnologist named Henry Christy,[65] who got him interested in studying the workings of human societies, or what Tylor would later call "the science of culture."

Together the two of them traveled to Mexico, where they spent three months. In 1861, Tylor published a book about their journey, *Anahuac: or, Mexico and the Mexicans, Ancient and Modern*—a travelogue sprinkled with his speculations on Mexican customs.

Back home, Tylor continued researching people who had not, as he saw it, reached civilization yet, and in 1871, he published his most famous work, *Primitive Culture: Researches into the Development of Mythology, Philosophy, Art, and Custom*. In it he laid out his definition of what the word "culture" meant. "Culture or Civilization," he wrote, "is that complex whole which includes knowledge, belief, art, morals, law, custom and any other capabilities and habits acquired by man as a member of society."[66]

According to Tylor, culture was a *quantity*, something that built up over time. Early humans were *savages* who had little. Their primitive culture was simple and emotionally rudimentary. Those who had risen to the next stage were *barbarians* who had accumulated a bit more knowledge and morals and manners. But those at the highest stage—by which he meant Europeans—had accrued the most. Their culture was pure and rational and scientific. They were civilized.

Tylor believed that all humans were the same species (this was a progressive idea at the time), and that we were all on the same path from an ignorant past to an enlightened future. In his eyes, the job of those who'd already reached civilization was to help others along the way.[67]

"[W]here barbaric hordes groped blindly, cultured men can often move onward with clear view," he wrote. "It is [the] office of ethnography to expose the remains of crude old culture which have passed into harmful superstition, and to mark these out for destruction."

"[T]he science of culture," he added, "is essentially a reformer's science."[68]

By the time I was in college in the 1990s, we knew that Tylor's definition of culture was wrong. Humans were one species, sure, but we were not all on the same path. There were many paths, many languages, and many patterns of human behavior—each of which arose in its own way in different parts of the world.

We were pluralists, or relativists, or multiculturalists. Or some mix of the three. We did not believe, as conservatives like William Bennett did, that there was one set of books and values and ideas that was superior to the rest.

Our line of thinking could be traced back to another towering figure in anthropology, the German academic Franz Boas, probably the second most important person in the history of the field after Tylor. Boas started out in the same school as Tylor, but as a young man he had an experience that would transform his way of thinking.

In 1881, when Boas was still a geography student, he traveled north to Baffin Island, near the Arctic Circle in Canada. His plan was to investigate how geography affected the natives' migration patterns.[69] He stayed for a year, all through Baffin's harsh winter. While he was there, something unexpected happened: Boas got to know the locals. He learned their language. He heard their stories. The Baffin natives opened up to him; he saw the sophistication of their way of life and their history. He saw how their lives and beliefs had been shaped by—and were suited to—the harsh world in which they lived.

When Boas returned home, he reached a startling conclusion—Tylor was wrong. The "savages" weren't so savage after all. "The more I see of their customs," he wrote in his journal, "[I find] we have no right to look down upon them."[70]

It wasn't that they hadn't yet acquired enough culture, or that they didn't have morals, or laws, or complex thoughts. The Baffin Islanders had all these things, but they were simply different from our versions of them, and they were hard to see unless you took the time and knew the language. Culture, he concluded, wasn't a single end point all humans were striving toward. It wasn't a mountaintop—it was a mountain range. Where Tylor saw *culture*, Boas began to see *cultures*.

Later, Boas went on to work among the Kwakiutl tribes of the Pacific Northwest,[71] and soon he came to reject the idea that humanity evolved in fixed "stages." Instead, he argued that cultures evolved independently and locally.

This realization was slowly dawning on Westerners everywhere. With the exploration, colonization, and mass migrations of the nineteenth and twentieth centuries, Europeans were encountering languages and lives and traditions and worlds with their own logics. They were meeting people with different understandings of the forces at work under the surface of things.

Yet the question of what culture actually was remained open. In the 1950s, anthropologists Alfred Kroeber and Clyde Kluckhohn tried to collect as many definitions of the word as they could, hoping to settle the question once and for all. They ended up with 164 descriptions, ranging from "all transmitted social learning" to "human energy organized in patterns of repetitive behavior" and "all products of organismic nongenetic efforts at adjustment."[72] In other words, no resolution at all.

By the beginning of the 1990s, the culture wars were at their peak, and cultural studies had become a hot academic field. But in spite of the prominence of the idea of culture (or at least the word), the effort to answer the simplest question— what is it?—remained maddeningly abstract.

It was around that time that Peter Logan, who teaches cultural studies at Temple University, started researching the history of the word "culture," tracing its roots through the culture wars, through the postmodern "cultural turn," through to E. B. Tylor, and beyond.

"It's a huge problem," Logan told me. "In all the discussions that I know of right now, nobody agrees what 'culture' means, even within cultural studies. There's an assumption that it can mean essentially anything, but that leads to problems, because if it means everything, it means nothing."

According to Logan, the main debate in cultural studies isn't over the question of one culture vs. many cultures, or even over which definition is the right one. Rather, it's "between people who think there should be a definition, and people who think there shouldn't." But even those who think there should can't decide what it would be.

One thing was clear: culture wasn't something only primitive people had, nor was it something only civilized people had. Culture wasn't education, nor was it ignorance. And it certainly wasn't just a bunch of random patterns passed down through the generations like an heirloom.

Culture was everywhere, but it was not everything. It wasn't biological, but it wasn't separable from biology. It was something powerful and fluid, something that got in us and became part of us. It was what made magical penis theft possible in one place and impossible in another. It was what made people on one side of a border, of a language, think differently and feel differently from those on the other side.

Knowing what it could do, however, didn't explain what it was, or where its power came from. And that's what I needed.

6

BAD BUNS

South and east of Hong Kong was another city that had once been plagued with retracting penises. In 1967, in one of the best-documented epidemics of *koro* ever, hundreds of people rushed to hospitals in the city-state of Singapore, deathly afraid that if they loosened their grip they would die.

Singapore today is one of the wealthiest and most successful countries on earth, and much of its old character seems to have been washed away by a tide of modernization. An international crossroads for hundreds of years, the city is now clean and safe and has everything most countries aspire to, even if, as a friend of mine put it, living in Singapore was like living in a doctor's waiting room.

How much had changed since 1967? Had the remains of the city's old culture been washed away, too? Were the old ways of thinking—of believing—gone? Or was it more complicated? How much had it changed, and how much had it stayed the same? The only way to find out if penises were still vanishing there was to go.

My first morning in the city, before the heat had come, I got up and took a bus along Orchard Road, which is now lined with glittering shopping malls. Near the end of the route, I got off at a tall, round building where a psychiatrist

named Paul Ngui had his practice. Ngui was one of the few
people still alive who had researched the 1967 epidemic.[73]

He was eighty-two years old, but he looked thin and fit.
He still golfed twice a week; he'd given up judo and boxing
and the other sports he used to do. He leaned forward and
handed me a copy of his paper, published when he was a
young doctor who took part in a study that followed up with
hundreds of *koro* patients.

"The epidemic was quite unusual," Ngui told me. "In the
past there were isolated cases around this region, especially
among the Chinese and Malays—maybe after sexual activity,
or masturbation of some kind. In this case, it's not linked to
any sexual activity, but to the eating of pork."

The epidemic began in October. In one case, a sixteen-
year-old male rushed into the General Hospital's outdoor
clinic with his parents close behind. As a report described it:
"The boy looked frightened and pale and he was pulling hard
on his penis to prevent the organ from disappearing into his
abdomen." His parents shouted for the doctors to help because
the boy had *suo yang*, and if he didn't stop the retraction he
would die. The doctors reassured the family and gave the boy
ten milligrams of chlordiazepoxide, after which he improved.

The boy's problem had started at school, where he'd heard
rumors that tainted pork—inoculated against swine fever—
could cause *koro*. Earlier that morning, he'd eaten a steamed
bun with pork in it. When he went to urinate, he looked down
and felt his penis start to shrink. "Frightened, he quickly grasped
the organ and rushed to his parents shouting for help."[74]

More people followed. Soon, the hospitals were flooded
with patients. Pork sales plummeted. The Ministry of Primary
Production announced that both swine fever and the vaccine
were harmless to humans, but the epidemic only seemed to

accelerate. For seven days it continued, until finally the Singapore Medical Association and the Ministry of Health started appearing on television and radio to announce that *koro* was a purely psychological condition, and that no one had died from it. There was an immediate drop in the number of cases, and by the end of the month, there were no reports at all.[75]

In the end, 469 cases were recorded,[76] though the real number was certainly higher, since the survey only included Western hospitals and did not account for traditional Chinese doctors. All patients who were interviewed by doctors had heard stories about *koro* before they experienced it. After the epidemic, the Chinese Physician Association concluded that "the epidemic of Shook Yang was due to fear, rumormongering, climatic conditions, and imbalance between heart and kidneys, and was in no way similar to the classical entity of Shook Yin."[77] (*Shook yang* is Cantonese for *suo yang*. *Shook yin* was sometimes used to refer to the condition that threatened both male and female gentalia.)[78]

Meanwhile, a Western-oriented "*Koro* Study Team," of which Ngui was part, concluded that *koro* was "a panic syndrome linked with cultural indoctrination."

"People would hear these rumors," Ngui told me, "and then they would have a bath or do something. And if they had a *cold* bath, then there would be some shrinking of the penis. And that would trigger the fear, because the belief was strong. Then they would rush to the hospital for treatment."

"Because they were afraid?" I asked.

"Yes. The fear. They had this tremendous fear. And you could see them clutching on to the penis, in the ambulance that was bringing them to the hospital in panic—the whole family in panic. And they believed, of course, that you can die, so there was this tremendous anxiety. It was usually the breadwinner, and they couldn't afford that. The local hospitals were overwhelmed by the numbers coming in. They just couldn't cope. But most of the people just required reassurance—or Valium."

The majority of the victims were Chinese, though a few were Malay and Indian. There were also a few cases of women who reported retraction of their genitals. Symptoms, besides retraction, included blurred vision, vomiting, collapse, and others. Most patients had some education, a few even had university degrees.[79] The authors of the *Koro* Study Group report wrote: "It may be too readily assumed that a culture-linked illness would be allied to superstitious belief which education would dispel."[80] And in his paper, Ngui wrote: "Cultural belief in the concept of *koro* is an important factor in its genesis."[81]

"These cultural beliefs were mainly from those Chinese who came from the south of China," Ngui told me. "Many of them have resettled in Singapore. They have come over many, many years before, from Fujian. When they came over, they still had a lot of these old cultural and traditional beliefs. There was more interest then in the Chinese education—the traditional learning of Chinese ancient history."

"And what about the strength of that belief today?"

"It is has gone down."

"But people still believe in yin/yang balancing, in traditional Chinese medicine?"

"Oh, yes, they do believe in that! But no more in *suo yang*," he said.

"Do you ever see cases of *amok*?" I asked.

"Not at all. You know, it's difficult to say, because in those days there were very few psychiatrists. And most of these cases were happening in very remote areas. One or two cases where people suddenly lose control and attack. In America, they have that too. Do they call it *amok*? They use guns there. But it's usually associated with some personality disorder, or disturbed history. We never got around to properly studying it, so we can't really say what *amok* means."

"And what about *latah*?"

"*Latah* is not a serious condition. It's more like a fun thing. I was from a Straits-born family, meaning Peranakan. You know Peranakan?"

"No."

"It means that my ancestors came from China and married with the Malays. The sons are sent to China to study. But because they are Malay, the mothers speak Malay to their children. My mother is Peranakan. My father is English-speaking Chinese, but we speak Malay at home. I can read Chinese, but we never got a Chinese education."

Ngui paused to check a message on his smartphone. Then he continued.

"In my family there was one *latah*—a cousin of mine. When the aunties and my mother's cousins got together, they would just poke him and sometimes he said swear words like 'fuck you' or 'vagina' or something like that. And everybody laughed. But he passed away maybe fifteen or twenty years ago. Now, you don't see it at all. But *latah* is not an illness. It is a syndrome. But it's not anxiety. It's just a reaction, a startle reaction."[82]

"And today, with the young people, there's no more *latah*?"

"No more. I don't hear of any."

"Do have any idea why?"

"I suppose they're all now educated. That's got a lot of do with it."

"And no more *koro*?"

"There are very, very few cases coming in. Our education system now is very good. I suppose most of these culture-bound syndromes will die off in time, no? I think they are dying out. We hardly see them anymore. So they will be relegated to history."

I thanked Ngui and said goodbye, then went back to the street and walked down Orchard Road. Here, again, was the question of education. Did that mark some difference between the past and present, ancient and modern? Walking along, I tried to imagine the distance between the Singapore of the thirty-six-year-old Ngui, interviewing terrified young men and their families, and the Singapore of the eighty-two-year-old Ngui, who never sees anything remotely like that anymore.

Singapore had changed, that much was clear. It was now a tourist town, a finance town, a shopping town. The Singapore River used to be lined with food hawkers selling meals for ten cents.[83] Today, theme restaurants sell drinks for $10. Where there were brothels and opium dens, there are now microbreweries and a Hooters.[84]

That evening I walked down to the water and sat on the steps of the quay. They were chipped and worn from 200 years of heavy use—most of Singapore's boat traffic used to load and unload there.

From my bag I dug out a can of Raffles beer I'd bought at Seven Eleven. Across the water I could see the statue of Sir Stamford Raffles himself—the founder of modern Singapore. I felt sure that the old world and the old ways couldn't be gone. Diluted, maybe, but not disappeared.

The sky was dark. Lightning flashed on the horizon. I raised my drink to Raffles and took a sip. Soon, all along the waterfront, the city's laser light show would begin.

• • •

Singapore's Chinatown is peppered with stores that sell traditional Chinese medicine. The next day I went there to ask around about *suo yang*. I strolled among the open bins of flattened squid, dried sea cucumbers, mushrooms, oysters, and tree bark. People streamed in constantly, bringing their health complaints, for which the shopkeepers could prescribe a mix of herbs and other ingredients—either fresh or prepackaged. All the stores did a brisk business.

In a dingy open-air mall packed with travel agencies, photocopy shops, noodle stands, and tea stores, I came to one of these places. I approached the counter. A portly man behind it ambled over. For some reason, I had my hand on stomach. He pointed to it.

"You have problem with bathroom?"

His English was limited, but he made a downward sweep with his hand that indicated the flushing of the bowels.

"Yes," I said. This was sort of true.

"You go every day?"

"Yes."

"Too many per day?"

I just kept saying yes. It seemed easier than launching into my genital inquiry.

"Is painful?"

"A little . . ." I lied.

He brought over a small box.

"You take this every day."

"Is this for yin or yang?"

"Oh you know yin and yang!"

"A little."

"This for too much yin."

"What other kinds of other things do you treat?"

"Many things!"

"Do you have anyone with *suo yang*?"

He stared blankly.

"*Suo yang*?" I said again. "When the man's penis is being sucked into his body?"

"No, never."

"You've been here for a long time?"

"This shop for fifty years. I am here thirty years."

"Were you here in 1967?"

"In 1967, I study."

I bought the stomach medicine, then walked around till I came to another shop. I asked the man working if he knew *suo yang*. "You know, when your penis is disappearing into your body." I tried to make the motions, but it was a strange public game of charades.

He pointed to his crotch. "You mean for this problem?"

"Yes."

"For men?"

"Yes."

He handed me a box of small pills. "This very good," he said. He turned away from the female clerks, lowered his elbow to his crotch and raised his forearm like a giant erection. "Makes you very strong."

"Thank you," I said, and I took the box from him an examined the label. This was not working. Language was a problem.

I put the medicine back, then went and called a friend who lived in the city, and who spoke and wrote Mandarin. He e-mailed me the Chinese characters for *suo yang* along with an explanation. I printed these out, then went back to Chinatown and stopped into the first shop I came to. I showed the woman at the country the paper.

"Do you know this?" I asked.

"Yes," she said. "One of the ingredients is *suo yang*. It's especially for men."

"No," I said, "it's not an ingredient. It's a condition. There was an epidemic and people thought they were going to die."

She looked at the paper. "To die? For this problem, maybe you should see the doctor."

"The traditional doctor?"

"Yes, he will be back in half an hour."

"But I don't need the medicine for myself."

"Here's some medicine. This will help you." She handed me a small box.

"How much is this?"

"Twenty dollars."

Back on the streets, I walked past the Chinatown museum,[85] past the crowd of tourists looking at drink menus. Despite appearances, and despite my communication troubles, it was clear that people had not stopped believing in the world as it was stitched together in old Chinese medical texts. Perhaps the difference was simply that now there was another world, the Western one, layered on top in a kind of palimpsest. How did they fit together? Was the older one weaker than before? I stopped in one last shop. The man working there wasn't particularly old but he spoke good English, so I asked him directly: "Do you ever have people ask about *suo yang*? When the penis is disappearing into the body?"

He knew exactly what I meant.

"For that," he said, "you need tiger penis. But it's very hard to get in Singapore. Maybe you go to Thailand."

"But do you get many people asking about it?"

"Not now. In the olden days, yes. But now, no."

"What would you do for them?"

"For that, you need to see your physician."

The next day, I got on a train and headed to the outskirts of town, to the campus of Singapore's Institute of Mental Health. It was a bigger, newer version of the old Woodbridge Hospital, where many victims of the 1967 epidemic had ended up, after it was decided their problems were mental, rather than genital.

Dr. Chee Kuan Tsee was a small man, mostly retired, but still active here. He too was one of the investigators into the 1967 epidemic. And now I sat across from him as he thought back on the time.

"I was only a little fry at that time," he said. "I was just doing my training. Paul Ngui was senior to me. I think there were about half a dozen of us on the investigative team. We set up a station in the clinics and we interviewed these people. That was a real epidemic, a real panic."

"Do you remember any of the people you interviewed?"

"I remember one man who was a university graduate. Normally we would associate this with the lower social class, not so well-educated, more superstitious. But we did have people with tertiary education. This man was from a Chinese university. And we had a Malay policeman. And you know he's a Muslim, and he doesn't eat pork, so he couldn't be infected by the pork. We also had a few cases—normally it's supposed to be a male disorder—but we did have a few females who complained of retracted vulva or retracted nipples."

"And what were they afraid of?"

"The main fear was death. You have other epidemics in Thailand and elsewhere, but I don't know the background explanation for other *koro* epidemics. They have their own stories, their own explanations for the phenomenon. But we have our own for the epidemic. Singapore is a dominant Chinese population, and 70 percent are Chinese, so belief in this *koro* has roots in traditional Chinese stories. One of them is the story of an emperor who died, and then people found that his penis had shrunken and retracted into his body. So the belief was that the shrunken or retracted penis would *cause* death, rather than because you are dead your penis shrinks, which will be the *effect* of death."

"Which emperor?" I asked.

"I can't remember. The principle investigator, Dr. Gwee Al Leng, was also a Chinese scholar, so he knew about this. But in Singapore, that would be the explanation for individual cases. In the Chinese population the shrinking penis is associated with death, which causes panic, anxiety. And that will be the explanation. But it doesn't explain everything."

"What do you mean?"

"Well, in mental disorders, there are many models and theories, but there's no single model to explain everything. The psychologist will think about the psychological model; the physician will think about the medical model; the social worker will think about the social model; the religious people will think about the religious model. So we try to look at it more holistically, more eclectically—"

"Don't they point to the same cause?"

"Well, in medicine, when you get a fracture or an infection or a heart blockage, those would be the so-called etiology—or the cause. But in psychiatry we don't have that, so the best we can do is with a syndrome—a cluster of symptoms that occur frequently together. They are given the name of some mental disorder. And who decides what syndromes will be called what mental disorders is a matter of consensus of

opinion, based on what experts all over the world decide: This
pattern, this progression, this cause, we will call it this mental
disorder.

"So it depends on how mighty you are and who has the
louder voice. At the moment the Americans have the loudest
voice. They just came out with the *DSM-IV* and *DSM-5* for
the whole world to follow. But they are not really scientific.
It's just that we think this is it. And it upsets a lot of developing countries that have a lot of syndromes that are so-called
culture-bound. They also tried to get into the *DSM*, but they
were pushed out because they said these are not scientific. In
India, they have even more culture-bound syndromes, but you
don't find them in *DSM*. They are excluded."

"So what is the cause?"

"You know we had this British psychiatrist, Max Hamilton. You know the Hamilton scale of anxiety and depression?
He came here many years ago—either late seventies or early
eighties. And we were quite annoyed with him. He was very
brash, very blunt. And we were talking about culture-bound
syndromes. And he brushed it all aside and said, 'These culture-bound syndromes, they are all rubbish.' He thought they
would be non-existent anymore. Everything would go down
to the basic psychopathology of anxiety, depression, psychosis,
and disassociated states.

"And in some ways he was correct. I don't see *amok*.[86] I
don't see *latah* any more. Even *koro* we hardly see now. So he
was correct in the sense that this globalized culture and life-
style—the globalized indoctrination—there's a lot of cloning.
And they can all be traced to the basic anxiety, depression,
psychosis and disassociated states. These are what he called the
'forms' of psychopathology. The form is the basis, the core. But
it's the manifestation which is the content. So delusion is the

form. But the manifestation of this will be different, and will be known as culture-bound. It would be influenced by what people are told about and what is expected from them. So it depends on the stories that have been handed down to them."

Just a mile or two north of where Dr. Chee and I sat was Singapore's northern border with Malaysia, a country that historically has had a huge influence on Singapore. In fact, Singapore was even part of the Malay Federation until it was kicked out in 1965.

Malaysia's cultural landscape is radically different from that of European countries, or even from that of the Chinese who came to dominate Singapore. And, as it happened, that country was the crucible of two of the best known culture-bound syndromes, *amok* and *latah*.

When I got back to the center of town, I crossed the Singapore River, walked past the old Malay cemetery, with its tiny headstones, and on to Kampong Glam—the Malaysian part of town. There was a beautiful old mosque, and across the street I found the Malay Heritage Center.

Inside, I sat for some time watching clips of old Malay horror films, which featured terrifying creatures I couldn't identify. There was also a display about traditional Malay medicine, which combines elements of Chinese medicine and ancient Greek *Yumani* medicine with other things like an elaborate ritual called *main peteri* meant to "weld back together" sick individuals. This ceremony predates Islam, and is still practiced in parts of Malaysia today. In it the *bomoh*—a witchdoctor, or traditional healer—performs exorcisms and trances and travels across the *maya*, or "veil of illusion," that separates the visible world from the invisible one.

At the front desk at the center, I found a helpful woman who told me a little about traditional Malay beliefs. She wore a headscarf and glasses.

"Do people still go to *bomohs*?" I asked.

"Oh!" she said. She looked around, alarmed. "*Bomoh* is a very strong word. You must be careful how you use it! There are different kinds of *bomohs*."

"What kinds?" I asked.

"First there is the traditional healer. They just try to help people. And then there is the kind that works with Satan. They use black magic."

"And it works?"

"Yes, it works! One of my friends—this is a life experience—one of my friends, her husband actually has a big company. So she thought, I want to marry someone else, and have boyfriend and things like that. So I actually went with her to many of the *bomohs*, and I saw that these things they were telling her are not right. And then she paid a Thai *bomoh* like three dollars so that something would happen to her husband."

"And did something happen to him?"

"No. She stopped, then her husband married someone else. When the spell is finished, you must keep paying them, or you get problems."

"In those movies in the other building, I saw a vampire-type thing. What is that?"

"That is *pontianak*, the female vampire."

"Is that the same as European vampires, where they drink your blood?"

"Very similar. But this is from generations. If your great-great-grandmother dies and becomes one, it is passed on to the next generation. Most vampires are people who die through suicide, or through accident. That's what my mother told me. They've never seen a male vampire, only the female vampire. They have long hair and white clothes because they come up from the grave. When you are walking to evening prayers they can get you."

"Do people still believe in that?"

"Mostly the old people. The young people, they are more educated now, so they don't believe it. Now they say it's nonsense, especially the vampires. They watch movies— they love horror movies about *penanggalan* [a flying vampiric head that has entrails dangling from its neck] in Singapore. Myself, I believe in all this, because at the end of the day, God created not only you, but even Satan and vampires and things like this. But that doesn't mean that I'm not afraid of them."

"Is that a traditional Malay belief?"

"Yes! You can get all this kind of information if you go to Indonesia. Singapore, it's a little more modern. Down there, though, you will see the *Orang Minyak*. The oil man."

"What is that?"

"The oil man actually has a collaboration with Satan. He had to sacrifice his mother's blood to Satan so he becomes a handsome man. Because the oil man is actually very ugly. But then he changed to be handsome. Another version says this *Orang Minyak* must rape one hundred women, then he can become a handsome rich man. Or something like that. It's so much of myth, but also fact. These things do happen.

"And one thing that is a little bit funny is that, if you see a female vampire, she may cut something on you, because you have what she doesn't have."

She smiled and gestured in a shy way toward the pelvic area.

"So they're looking for men?"

"Yes. Or revenge."

"I see." It was getting late. The sun was on its way down. "So I should hurry home?"

"Yes," she said. "Perhaps."

7

AMERICAN MALADIES

It was a strange feeling to sit across from people like Paul Ngui and Dr. Wai, and to have them tell me that education, Westernization, and modernization were the things extinguishing the cultural syndromes. The unspoken assumption in all this was the superiority—the rationality—of European culture.

This was like Tylor turned on his head, because if they were right, it would mean that education marked a kind of elimination of culture, rather than the attainment of it. If that were so, it would mean our American syndromes are culture-free . . . and, by implication, we are, too.

I knew this wasn't true. We have a culture. From the inside it isn't always easy to see, but I'd been pulled in and out of it enough times to know for sure. Whenever I came back from overseas, I felt its strangeness as palpably as the day I landed in Italy, or Nigeria, or Thailand. I'd arrive and feel like an anthropologist examining a race of people who ran in circles, who thought bulging muscles were beautiful, and who saw convenience as a kind of birthright.

Of course we had a culture. And if we had a culture, we had to have cultural syndromes—conditions unique to us, which didn't occur elsewhere. But these weren't listed in the back of the *DSM*. Some of them were included in the main body of the manual, like anorexia, while others were mentioned elsewhere: repressed memory syndrome, Truman syndrome, type-A personality, pet hoarding.

These were syndromes that other people did not have; they were mental conditions that fed off our loneliness; our obsessions with thinness, with youth, with celebrity, with vulnerability. They were fueled and shaped by the things we believed.

One day, in the midst of my research, I was talking to Bridgit when she said, "Well, I got my period. I guess that explains my mood."

I shrugged and asked: "Or does it?"

This was followed by an icy silence. Because the only thing worse than diagnosing PMS is suggesting it might be a cultural syndrome.

"Never mind," I said. "We'll go with 'It does.'"[87]

But I couldn't help myself. For the last few days I'd been reading fascinating research about Premenstrual Syndrome, the bulk of which suggested that it wasn't caused by a tide of hormones wreaking havoc on a woman's psyche.

The basic idea of PMS (that a woman can't overcome her body) can be traced back 2,500 years to Hippocrates, the father of Western medicine, who believed that certain moods and physical disorders in women were caused by "hysteria" or the "wandering uterus," meaning the organ literally drifted around the body, pulled by the moon, lodging in wrong places, blocking passages, causing pressures. Cures included marriage and intercourse.[88]

This notion endured for eons. But by the early 1900s, medical theories around "hysteria" were beginning to crumble. In 1908, at the meeting of the *Societé de Neurologie* in Paris, Joseph Babinski argued that hysteria was "the consequence of suggestion, sometimes directly from a doctor, and more often culturally absorbed."[89]

Today, hysteria is never diagnosed, except by unwise husbands.

In 1931, however, an American gynecologist named Robert Frank revived the idea in a new guise. He published an article titled, "The hormonal causes of premenstrual tension." Frank described symptoms that occurred in the week before menstruation: irritability, bloating, fatigue, depression, attacks of pain, nervousness, restlessness, and the impulse for "foolish and ill considered actions," due to ovarian activity. Again, the cause was the uterus.[90]

Then in 1953, British physician Katharina Dalton elaborated on this, arguing the condition came from fluctuation of estrogen and progesterone. She called it Premenstrual Syndrome,[91] and soon symptoms grew to include: anxiety, sadness, moodiness, constipation or diarrhea, feeling out of control, insomnia, food cravings, increased sex drive, anger, arguments with family or friends, poor judgment, lack of physical coordination, decreased efficiency, increased personal strength or power, feelings of connection to nature or to other women, seizures, convulsions, asthma attacks, not to mention flare ups in asthma, allergies, sinusitis, anxiety disorders, irritable bowel syndrome, migraines, and multiple sclerosis.[92]

If any of these symptoms occurred in the second half of the menstrual cycle, one had PMS. Estimates of the number of women afflicted ranged from 5 percent to 95 percent.[93]

In the 1980s, three women in the UK were tried for arson, assault and manslaughter. The three all claimed they had diminished responsibility due to PMS, and got reduced sentences on the condition that they underwent hormone treatment.[94]

After that, according to one study, American women flooded doctors with requests for help with their PMS. "Popular groups like PMS Action were founded to promote recognition and treatment of PMS by medical professionals. Private PMS clinics began to appear in the USA, modeled after those in the UK, and progesterone therapy was enthusiastically adopted, much to the chagrin of many gynaecologists who viewed its use as 'unscientific' and 'commercial', not to mention unlicensed."[95]

Based on all this, the 1987 version of the *DSM-III* included a new category: Late Luteal Phase Disorder (*luteal* refers to progesterone). It was proposed as a topic for further research, but despite the absence of such research, it was included in the 1994 edition of the *DSM-IV* under the name Premenstrual Dysmorphic Disorder, or PMDD.[96] In 2013, in the *DSM-5*, it was given its own category as a full-fledged mental illness.[97]

Yet neither PMS nor PMDD occur in most cultures.[98] There are no biomarkers to measure them by. No conclusive correlation has ever been found between estrogen or progesterone levels and PMS.

As one study noted, "the more time that women of ethnic minorities spend living in the United States, the more likely they are to report PMDD. Thus, if we are to accept PMDD as a reified medical disorder, then we must also accept exposure to U.S. culture as a risk factor for contracting PMDD."[99]

If it is a syndrome at all, it's a cultural one.[100]

None of this would have surprised Lynn Payer, a medical reporter who grew up in Kansas. She studied biochemistry and physiology before going on to journalism school, graduating in 1969. Not long after that, she moved to France, where she lived for eight years and worked as a health correspondent and editor for *The New York Times*. In France, she noticed that when she went to the doctor she got wildly different advice than her doctors in the United States.

At first, as she wrote in her book, *Medicine and Culture*, she thought this was because, "European doctors were less well educated than those in the United States, that their medicine was more 'primitive.' As an American with a background in biochemistry, I believed medicine to be a science with a 'right' and 'wrong' way to treat a disease, and any deviation from the American norm to be 'wrong.'"[101]

In France, however, she began to encounter conditions that didn't exist in America or anywhere outside France. If you went in to a doctor complaining about a migraine, there was a good chance you'd be diagnosed with *crise de foie*, or "liver crisis" for which you could get any number of drugs. If you showed symptoms of fatigue, muscle cramps, or hyperventilation, you might be diagnosed with "spasmophilia" and get treated for that.

Other countries had their own maladies. In Germany, if you had low blood pressure, you would be diagnosed with *Herzinsuffizienz* or "heart insufficiency," and given heart medication, of which Germans took far more than any other nationality in the world. In England, people were frequently diagnosed with "chilblains," or blotchy red patches caused by constriction of blood vessels due to cold—a condition rarely seen outside of England.[102]

"Often," Payer wrote, "all one must do to acquire a disease is to enter a country where that disease is recognized—leaving the country will either cure the malady, or turn it into something else."

America, Payer noted, has a highly mechanistic understanding of the body. This is known as the "biomedical model," and in our version, we view the body as a machine.[103]

We see our circulatory system as plumbing. We see the brain as a computer. We see our heart as a pump. We think of the body as a car—a metaphor that dates back to the 1920s, when cars first entered our lives.

Likewise, we see the doctor as a mechanic, and illness as the result of a part breaking, which it's the doctor's job to repair. If something can't be explained in mechanical terms, we tend not to believe it's real. And yet, things are often more complicated than that.

Take carpal tunnel syndrome. Most of us believe this is a purely biomechanical condition: We use a computer too much, hold our wrists the wrong way, and a nerve rubs on a bone. A problem ensues.

But oddly, several conditions nearly identical to carpal tunnel syndrome have come and gone in the past. In the 1830s doctors began to report cases of "writers' cramp," or "scriveners' palsy," which afflicted an emerging class of clerical workers. They too experienced pain, paralysis, numbness, aching, spasms and stiffness in their hands and wrists, and a "multiplicity of symptoms that could affect workers in unpredictable ways."[104] The condition disappeared in the late 1800s.

In 1875, a new condition emerged in the *British Medical Journal*: "telegraphists' cramp," which caused numbness, stiffness, pain and similar conditions to writers' cramp. In 1894, one expert estimated that the condition affected 0.5 percent of operators. By 1911, a study in Britain found that it affected 64 percent of operators.[105] Then, a few years later, both the telegraph and its cramp were gone. The case was closed.

Despite the widespread use of typewriters and pens throughout the twentieth century, there were no new hand/wrist syndromes reported until the 1980s, when workers in the meatpacking industry began coming down with "cumulative trauma syndrome," or carpal tunnel syndrome, with symptoms identical to writers' and telegraphists' cramps.

Union newspapers published articles about the dangers of the condition. It became a flashpoint in labor disputes, as workers were being downsized and automated. Union activists worked to raise awareness of the problem. Media outlets reported on the epidemic even as it grew. Soon "the problem of occupational hand and wrist disorders had migrated to a host of other industries, particularly auto assembly, textiles, apparel manufacturing, electronics and newspaper publishing," wrote Allard Dembe in his study of the condition.[106]

At the same time, Australia was seeing a different pattern. The country had also seen a spike in the number of workers reporting what they called "repetitive strain injuries." But in 1985, cases plummeted after the Supreme Court ruled it was not a legitimate compensation issue. This prompted an outpouring of opinion suggesting that RSI was primarily psychosomatic, or psychological, not biomechanical.[107]

In either case, repetitive, strenuous movements were part of the cause but not all of it. Dembe points out other factors in all these conditions: the use of new technologies, social and economic anxiety, media stories about the dangers of repetitive movements and so on.

Carpal tunnel syndrome can't be explained in purely mechanical terms because, like PMS and liver crisis and anorexia and so many other illnesses, it is partly shaped by something in our culture, so it rises and falls with those tides. Since concern about carpal tunnel syndrome has dropped in the United States, so have the number of cases, with a 21 percent decrease in 2006 alone. Keyboards, nonetheless, remain in high demand.

•   •   •

The shortcoming of our mechanistic model is something we've barely begun to come to grips with. For example, when the *DSM-5* was released in 2013, Thomas Insel, the director of the National Institutes of Mental Health wrote: "Mental disorders are biological disorders involving brain circuits that implicate specific domains of cognition, emotion, or behavior." He lamented the fact that when the NIMH set out to determine the biological parameters of these disorders, "It became immediately clear that we cannot design a system based on biomarkers or cognitive performance because we lack the data."[108]

The assumption was that we haven't found biological tests for mental disorders because we haven't looked hard enough. That is possible. Yet it's also possible we lack the data because we're looking in the wrong places.

"The scandal of psychiatry," Arthur Kleinman told me when I called to ask about this, "is that with fifty years of biological research, we've failed to come up with a single biological test that can be used routinely to diagnose patients. Depression, anxiety, schizophrenia—any common psychiatric disorder. It's a scandal because that's where most of the research money has gone. The research money has not advanced the field nearly as much as was hoped clinically."[109]

Why is that? Is it because the best minds at the best universities in the world, with the most money for research, simply don't know where to look? Or is there some piece missing, something else that happens at a level above the cellular one? Is the reason these conditions don't show up on a functional MRI because they are partly cultural? Is it because they are partly psychogenic? Is it because they emerge—in part—from the way we view ourselves and the world?

I have always been puzzled by the fact that mental illnesses occur at different rates around the world. Panic attacks happen everywhere, but they occur in 11.2 percent of people in the United States and only 2.7 percent in Germany. The number of people with Panic Disorder is 4.9 percent in the United States, but only 0.1 percent in Nigeria. Social anxiety disorder averages a 4.8 percent rate in the United States, but only 0.2 percent in metropolitan China and 49.4 percent in Udmurtia, a region in the Russian Federation.[110]

Depression is another example. In America, most people believe depression is the result of a biochemical imbalance, and that the way to fix it is to apply more chemicals. Yet rates of depression also vary across the world; Korea, Taiwan, and Puerto Rico have low levels of depression (less than 5 percent), while in France, Switzerland, and the United States, the levels range between 15 percent and 20 percent.[111] Asian countries tend to have less than European countries.[112] In Korea or Japan, you have a one in fifty chance of suffering major depression in a year. In Brazil, you have a one-in-ten chance.[113] Lifetime prevalence of major depression varies from 6.5 percent in China, to 9.8 percent in South Africa, to 19.2 percent in the United States.[114] A meta-analysis of studies on postpartum depression across forty countries found prevalency ranging from 0 percent to 60 percent.[115]

These kinds of comparisons are tricky, because of language differences,[116] and because ideas about the body and mind (and spirit) vary widely from country to country. Yet even something as clearly defined as schizophrenia varies greatly: In 1992, a major multiyear study by the World Health Organization found that patients in India, Nigeria, and Colombia had a milder form of the disease and better recovery rates than sufferers in the United States, Denmark, and Taiwan. In the richer countries, 40 percent of sufferers

were severely impaired, while in the less industrialized countries, only 24 percent were.[117]

It seems that Payer was right, and that crossing a border
might affect the kinds of illnesses you get. One study showed
the lifetime prevalence (meaning at least once in your life) of
any mental illness varied from 12.2 percent in Turkey, to 20.2
percent in Mexico, to 37.5 percent in Canada, to 48.6 percent
in the United States.[118]

All of these conditions appear to be not just biological,
but *biocultural*, which is to say, they are shaped by both biology and culture. This is not the same as saying they aren't real.
It's saying that, while there is biology at work, there are other
links in the chain.

What, then, is the link between biology and culture?
What would make one group of people more depressed, more
anxious, than another? What makes one people feel like their
necks are exploding, another like their penises are vanishing,
another like their livers are having a crisis, and another like
their wrists are hardening from the inside out?

One summer night in 1968, my grandmother Irene woke up,
opened a bottle of barbiturates, and swallowed them all. She
then climbed back into bed. The next morning my grandfather found her body next to his. She was fifty-six years
old. They had been married since she was sixteen and he was
nineteen.

At the time, my father was away in New York, stationed
at West Point Military Academy, where he played in the band.
My grandfather called him to give him the news. Now, almost
fifty years later, he still has to compose himself when he talks
about that day. All his dad said was "Mom's gone."

He knew what this meant. He was devastated, but he wasn't surprised. Growing up, he'd watched my grandmother struggle with depression. She would lie in bed for days, then she'd be away at a hospital for weeks at a time. Once, she pushed a screen from an upper-story window and fell out, landing on the driveway. She was bruised and alive, but she wished she weren't.

My grandparents were born into a community of Czech immigrants in a small Iowa town. Her life there was a hard one: Her mother treated her so cruelly that, even as an adult, she often wondered if she'd been adopted.

My grandfather grew up across the street. As a teenager, he fell hard for Irene, and they eloped. My father believes they had some good years early on, but the good times soon receded. Their marriage was not a happy one. My grandfather was inflexible and cold to her. She often wondered aloud if he loved her. She wanted more than anything to own a house, but when she found one and put a down payment on it without telling him, he was livid and made her get the money back. They rented for the rest of their lives.

I didn't know any of this until I was much older. To me, my grandfather was a warm old man who clearly loved us. He joked and bought us weird toys from mail order catalogs. He was good to my father and my mother. All I knew about my grandmother was that she died because she had been "sick."

Eventually, the story began to trickle out. This happened, I think, because for my father the idea of my grandmother being sick and the idea that she had killed herself had merged into one. She was depressed. Depression was a disease. And the disease caused her death.

At the time, our whole culture's notion of depression was undergoing a similar transformation. It was a sea change from the times my grandmother grew up in, when depression was blamed on personal weakness, and suicide was viewed as a coward's choice or worse: a sin. There were laws against it, and in some states, if a person committed suicide, the government could seize the heirs' inheritance.

In her life, there had been no language to talk about what was wrong with my grandmother, and there was no real help for her. She was diagnosed with depression or said to have had a "nervous breakdown," but the results were always the same: at the hospitals my grandfather took her to, all they could do was give her sleeping pills. In spite of his harshness, my grandfather tried everything to help her, but nothing could. In the end it became clear he'd loved her more than anyone—even she—had known.

Since the 1960s, as our understanding of depression shifted from something "mental" to something "physical," it also shifted from being something *imaginary* to something *real*. This change came about largely because of the success of drugs like Prozac, which seemed to help people almost magically, by tinkering with their serotonin levels. By the early 2000s, depression was understood in almost purely biochemical terms.

For my father, I believe, this was both a relief and a kind of revelation. It made his mother's death easier to accept. It absolved her of wrongdoing. It removed her agency and removed his doubt. Because if depression is a brain disease, if it is physical, it is tangible. It is real. No one blames a person when their heart stops. No one blames a person when they get skin cancer. (Which is a condition my father knows a lot about—he's a dermatologist.) Yet people did blame his mother, even though she was broken inside, too.

But to me, the biomedical explanation of depression

never rang completely true.[119] Over the years, I'd started to question the stark division between mental and physical, real and imaginary. Because if depression were a purely biochemical process, it would be more consistent—it wouldn't vary over time, or from culture to culture. That didn't mean, of course, that depression wasn't real. Only that there had to be more to the story.

In a 2013 editorial in the *British Journal of General Practice* entitled "Depression as a culture-bound syndrome," the psychiatrist Christopher Dowrick, author of *Beyond Depression*, argued that our beliefs about happiness were contributing to its absence. "From a cultural perspective, in Western anglophone societies we have developed an ethic of happiness, within which aberrations from the norm are assumed to indicate illness." He noted that depression was increasing at a rate that made it "destined to become the second most disabling disease by 2020."[120]

This ethic of happiness was something I knew well. It was one of the facets of America that struck me most whenever I returned from abroad. The quest for happiness informs every aspect of our lives: our movies have happy endings, our books tell us how to maximize happiness. We've turned the science of happiness into an industry. We *expect* to be happy—or at least to achieve happiness—at some point in our lives. And in that environment—that culture—feelings of unhappiness take on the added weight of failure, of wrongness, of illness. When we are not happy, we feel like something is broken.

In other cultures, being happy and having positive feelings are not considered a normal, everyday state of mind. Feeling depressed is thus not considered abnormal. Russians, for example, don't feel like they need to be happy all the time. A study of American and Russian students found that while

Russians tended to focus on "dark feeling and memories," they were "less likely than Americans to feel as depressed as a result." The study's co-author, Igor Grossmann, said: "Among Westerners, focusing on one's negative feelings tends to impair well-being, but among Russians, that is not the case." They didn't expect to be happy, and so were less bothered when they weren't.[121]

Depression, or something like it, occurs in every culture. But rates differ and symptoms vary. Culture shapes depression, moderates depression, aggravates depression and changes depression. This means that depression isn't entirely biochemical either, but biocultural. There is biology at work, but there is also something else.

All of which makes me wonder about my grandmother. What if she'd felt more love from her mother? What if she'd had different ideas, different beliefs, different expectations about what her life should be? What if she'd lived a life more like the one she wanted or had a different understanding of her own sorrow? For that matter, what if everyone around her had had a different understanding, as well? If any of those things changed, would her road have been more bearable?

In 1998, Charles Hughes, co-editor of *Culture-Bound Syndromes: Folk Illnesses of Psychiatric and Anthropological Interest*, wrote a scathing critique of the *DSM-IV*'s treatment of culture-bound syndromes. He argued that "[t]o use the class-designated term 'culture-bound [psychiatric] syndromes' is comparable to using the terms 'culture-bound religion,' 'culture-bound language,' or 'culture-bound technology,' for each of these institutional areas is shaped by, and in its specific details is unique to, its cultural setting."[122]

Koro and its kin might languish at the back while other conditions such as depression, multiple personality disorder, bulimia, muscle dysmorphia, and premenstrual dysmorphic disorder were granted universal status because Western psychiatrists couldn't see beyond their own cultural horizons. In reality, everything else in the *DSM*, and in life, is culture-bound.[123]

"My own feeling," Arthur Kleinman told me, "is that we're in an age where we should give up the idea of culture-bound syndromes. *All* syndromes carry some degree of cultural influence, some more than others. But what happened with the culture-bound syndromes is that they came to reflect syndromes that don't make immediate sense in the context of the United States and Western Europe—which make up fewer than 20 percent of the world's population. As if the others were all culture-bound and the 20 percent that happen to be in the United States and Europe were culture-free. And that's complete nonsense."[124]

Which means, in a sense, that all our maladies are culture-bound. But it's in our own syndromes where we can begin to see what it is they are bound to.

8

MINGLING MEDICINES

Night was falling as our train rolled into the People's Republic of China. I had some reservations about this branch of my journey. I was going to a country I'd never been to, where I knew no one, and where I spoke not a word of the language. But I knew that I wanted to get beyond the bright lights of Hong Kong and the clean surfaces of Singapore into rougher territory. I suspected that if I could get past the wall of language, I might find other worlds, other cultures, that had endured and even thrived—places where *koro* might exist.

There was no better place to start this search than in Guangzhou, where Dr. Wai said the 1967 Hong Kong *koro* epidemic had begun. Historically, Canton—the colonial name for Guangzhou—had been China's window to the world. It was one of the earliest ports visited by Europeans, and in the old days there was even a saying: "Everything new begins in Canton."[125]

The train pulled into the city late at night and connected to the new subway system. I went to the touch-screen ticket kiosk and followed the instructions to the end: "Please put cashes into."

I put my cashes into, then sped across town to a hostel called the "Lazy Gaga." It was painted bright yellow and full of foreigners in town for the Canton Fair, a kind of trade show for bit players in the global economy. As at my hostel in Hong Kong, everyone sat staring at their laptops, except for a few outliers. An overweight Turk sat on the couch watching movies, while in another corner a Polish backpacker bent over his bicycle, tools strewn around, as he tried to mount a small motor in it, and swearing loudly about the cheap Chinese production. When I got into the elevator, a young Chinese woman thrust her business card at me. I thanked her, put it in my pocket, and let her assume I was another minor industrialist.

Upstairs I found my room. It had two bunk beds. I took a bed over one occupied by a middle-aged, gray haired Italian man who owned a small company, for which he needed parts manufactured. On the bottom bunk of the other bed was a young Chinese programmer from the north, who had been recruited to work for a local company, but who hated his job and was thinking about quitting.

The next morning, downstairs in the lobby, I was standing at the front desk talking to Yau, the smart, funny, slightly disheveled owner of the Lazy Gaga. Yau always seemed to have a million things going on, and he was constantly digging in his fanny pack for something. He spoke excellent English and we chatted about the building, which, he said, had been built in 1982 as a government hotel—the first in the area with an elevator.

"Back then," Yau said, "people used to come around to see the elevator but were scared to ride it."

The hotel went bankrupt around 2000. He bought the building cheaply, because a building next door had constructed apartments that extended out *over* the roof of the hostel. (This quirk had earned it a spot in a CNN story about Chinese zoning laws, he said.)[126]

I told Yau what I was working on, and showed him my piece of paper with "*suo yang*" written on it in Chinese. I told him I was researching mental illnesses that occurred only in certain cultures.

He looked at the paper. "But it's not a mental condition, is it?" he asked "It's just a symptom. There are a variety of reasons a man's genitals can shrink."

"Really?"

"Yes! We used to see the kung fu movies where they would say '*shook yang*' to protect their genitals."

I thanked him, wrote that down in my notebook, then asked if he knew any translators. He agreed to make some calls, and later tracked down a young art student named Shirley who could translate as I walked around town trying to ask about penis shrinkage.

The next day, Shirley met me at the Lazy Gaga. She was from Guangzhou, and from the middle class. Both her parents owned factories (her mother's made 3D glasses for movie theaters). But she had no interest in the family trades. Her passion was art. She showed me her work on her smart phone, and she was clearly talented. Plus, her English was excellent.

We sat down and I explained all about *suo yang*, which she'd never heard of. I handed her some of the research papers and she read them with curiosity and the occasional chuckle.

"So, do you think it's real, this thing? Or is it just something they imagine?"

"I don't know," I said, fumbling for the words I hadn't yet settled on. "Maybe for the people who feel it, it's real to them."

Shirley had some ideas about where to go to see if there were still cases of *koro* in the area, and we set off across the city together. It was mid-morning. The streets pulsed with cars and electric bikes. The shops seemed like they were filled with nothing but wholesalers, all of whom had their wares on display: shoes, hardware, purses, textiles.

Guangzhou had around 14 million people and was considered China's third-most important city, though it struggled to be known as anything more than a giant factory. In 2010, when the Asian Games were held there, the city started on a spate of high-profile developments. This included the 2,000-foot-tall Canton Tower, whose bold, parabolic shape "makes it seem like a lady looking behind with full passion and emotion," according to one description.[127] It was a strange and beautiful structure befitting a strange and beautiful city.

We came to a wide, busy road and got on a bus to the Guangzhou University of Traditional Chinese Medicine Hospital. In the lobby Shirley made some inquiries as to where we should ask about *suo yang*.

We climbed up a few flights of stairs to the urology department. This seemed noteworthy, because if *suo yang* were a mental problem, shouldn't we be in the psychiatry department? Maybe it was considered a bodily affliction after all.

Down a long, echoing hall, we passed many people with urinary problems until we got to the office of Dr. Li Xing Ping. He seemed baffled by the sudden arrival of a foreigner, but recovered quickly as he welcomed us in.

Shirley explained the situation, and Dr. Li nodded. She translated my questions and his answers.

"Is *suo yang* common?" I asked. "Do many people come to ask about this?"

"No," he said, "it is very rare."

"So in a year, maybe how many people do you see with it?"

"Maybe none."

"In the past, was it more common?"

"Not really," he said. "In the big city it's rare, but in the rural areas, you can see it. It's more like a mental thing."

"And if someone came with this, what would you advise them?"

"I would tell them to calm down and take their hands off their penis, because they are so anxious and keep grabbing it because they are so afraid it will retract. And if that's not helping, I would give him some medical things, to calm him."

"Like herbs?"

"Yes."

Dr. Li motioned behind us and called in his next patient, which meant that it was time for us to go. We thanked him and left his office.

Back on the street, we took another bus to the Guangdong Provincial Hospital of Traditional Chinese Medicine—a twenty-nine-story building that was actually around the corner from the Lazy Gaga on a leafy street full of hardware dealers. The hospital had been founded in 1924[128] and had grown ever since, even as the government mandated the integration of Chinese and Western medicines. As the website put it, the hospital would "continue to pursue the highest level of Chinese medicine treatment, continue to pursue the forefront of modern medical treatment, and strive to make the perfect combination of both."[129]

The lobby gleamed like an airport. The air smelled rich and herbal. Along the edge of the hall was a row of touch screen kiosks where patients selected their ailment, found a doctor, and made an appointment.

We walked over to the machines, where a young technician had one open and was making repairs. He explained the system. When Shirley told him what we were looking for, he laughed and covered his mouth.

As it happened, you needed a card to swipe to make an appointment. Since we didn't have one, he swiped his own, found a urologist, and handed us a number.

On the fifth floor, we sat in the waiting area, looking for our number and the photo of our doctor on the screen. The waiting area was packed. On the wall was a list of the kinds of medicine practiced behind that desk: neurosurgery, gastrointestinal surgery, vascular surgery, thyroid surgery, hepatopancreatobiliary surgery, andrology, and, of course, urology.

Our number came up on the screen. We walked up to the desk, and Shirley explained. The nurse pointed back to the office, where we met a doctor who didn't give us his name.

Once again, Shirley translated.

"Have you seen any people with *suo yang*?" I asked.

"No, not many."

"In a year, maybe?"

"Three or four."

"And do they feel like it's a dangerous thing, or just a minor thing?"

"The patients get anxious when they have this. They are very nervous."

"Anxious that they might die?"

"No. They worry about their sexual abilities."

"And so what treatment do you give them?"

"Usually Chinese herbs for relaxing and the penis will be better."

"So it's not serious?"

"No, not serious, but with older people, maybe it is more difficult."

That was it. Again we thanked the doctor and left.

Shirley walked me back to the Lazy Gaga, where we parted ways. That night I sat on a plastic chair down the street from the hostel and ate seafood and mushrooms grilled on a fire. I watched the smoke rise up into the darkness and get carried away by the wind, and I thought about all the unseen currents flowing around me.

The next day, I took the subway to a quiet part of town—the final place I wanted to visit in Guangzhou. I walked down a tree-lined street where vendors had spread their goods on blankets on the sidewalk. They were covered with old things: coins, pipes, medals. Flotsam that washed up here from the past.

Eventually I came to the sign I was looking for. It said, "Guangzhou Brain Hospital," in English. It was the oldest mental hospital in China, founded in 1898 by an American named John Glasgow Kerr.[130] The investigators of the 1984 Hainan epidemic had come from here, and I hoped that I might find someone who knew about it, or even remembered working on it.

There didn't seem to be a reception area, so I wandered through the campus before I came to a small park-like area with two statues, one of Kerr, and another of Dr. Mo Kan-Ming—the lead investigator of the Hainan epidemic. He'd died in 1996 at the age of eighty.

Across the park I saw what looked like an administrative center of some kind. I went in, climbed the stairs, and stopped in the first office. A young man was sitting at his desk. I showed him the study of the epidemic, and asked if any of the authors were still around.

He stared at the names. He read them out loud in halting English. He said a few were dead. The others he didn't know. I asked if there was anyone else researching this, and he motioned for me to follow him. We walked down the hall to the office of Dr. Li Jie, an energetic man who invited me in and was very excited to hear what I was doing. He jumped up, rushed over to a file cabinet, and pulled out a paper titled "*Koro* endemic among school children in Guangdong, China," about an outbreak that took place in a village south of Guangzhou called Fuhu.[131] It read:

> In the late afternoon of May 21, 2004, a third-grade boy student, after playing ping-pong, felt that his penis was shrinking, began to panic, and ran home to tell his parents. His anxious mother held the boy's penis, while his father immediately called a local healer, an 80-year-old lady, for emergency treatment.

The old lady treated the boy with "moxibustion,"[132] and his symptoms went away. But then:

> Two days later, on May 23, when the school principal learned about the incident, he gathered all the students (393 boys and 287 girls, 680 in total) together in the school courtyard. Using a microphone, the principal explained to the students in detail what had happened, and warned them to be cautious, and to take emergency measures if they experienced similar symptoms.

That day, several boys felt their penises shrinking and rushed home to get treatment. The following day, sixty more students were struck with *suo yang*. All except for one were treated by the healer. When Dr. Li interviewed her, she recalled a previous epidemic in 1963, caused by "a change in the government order [the Great Leap Forward, a massive and devastating campaign of industrialization and collectivization], bringing an "evil wind" that intruded into people's bodies."

> She believed that suoyang tended to occur when there was a cold wind, manifested as wind sickness. She further mentioned that this illness condition should not be treated by Western medicine, such as injections, or it would result in death. It should only be treated with the traditional method of aijiu, or moxibustion, plus drinking water with chili powder (yang element) to warm the stomach and kidneys.

In 2009, Li and his colleagues went back to the village to give a "Folk Belief Questionnaire." Among Fuhu's adults, 57 percent believed *suo yang* was a dangerous condition. Among children, 59 percent did. At that time, the belief was still very strong.[133]

"Is this still going on?" I asked Dr. Li. "Are there still epidemics? Or is this the only one?"

"That's the only one," he said, "I think it is usually in villages that are poor and not well educated. Since 2009, there has not been an epidemic of *koro* in the south of China. *Koro* is rare now. Very rare. Sometimes in the clinic, you can find one person, maybe, who is suffering from *koro*. We had one high school student, nineteen years old, who is suffering from *koro* in 2009. But I think *koro* has become more and more rare."

"But people still believe in traditional Chinese medicine?"

"Yes. Some people believe traditional Chinese medicine is very good. But it is an art, not a science. It is a philosophy. And since the twenty-first century, this phenomenon of epidemics has greatly disappeared. Maybe because of the economic, social development. And the education. Globalization.

One world. One culture. So *koro* has disappeared. Why do you want to study these epidemics?"

"I was in Hong Kong—" I started to explain, but he interrupted.

"Ah! Yap Pow Meng was from Hong Kong! I remember his work. He was very famous."

"Are there any patients from 1985 who could tell what it was like?"

Li thought, then shook his head. "No, I don't think so."

"Are any of these people around, these doctors?" I handed him the paper.

"Dr. Mo Kan-Ming, he was our boss," Li said. "But he is passed along. Dr. Tseng—also he is my friend, but he passed along too. Most of them are dead. This one, he retired, maybe last year, but I don't know where he is."

"Would it be possible to go to Fuhu?"

"Maybe. It is twenty or fifty kilometers from Yanjiang to Fuhu. Maybe you can call Dr. Peng Xinxin. He works near Yanjiang. Then maybe you can take a bus to Fuhu."

That sounded like a lot of maybes. But he gave me Dr. Peng's phone number. I thanked him and left.

One thing I knew: I needed to go south, where old winds blew.

The train started out of Guangzhou. It felt good to be moving. I'd left the Lazy Gaga that morning and was now on my way down the peninsula to Zhanjiang, a city of several million people and the northernmost border of the 1985 epidemic, which traveled up the peninsula. (There was a smaller outbreak outside the city in 1987, too.) Several times I tried to call Dr. Peng, but there was no answer.

Out the window, I watched high, jagged mountains roll by. The train was filled with loud talking. We passed through small towns and rice fields, saw nuclear power plants and half-built mansions. There were pig farms and fish farms and cell phone towers. The mountains were shrouded in mist. Guangzhou's jungle of skyscrapers seemed distant already.

After several hours, the train stopped. I turned to the woman next to me and showed her my ticket.

"Zhanjiang?" I asked.

She nodded and pointed to the door. I rushed down the aisle and got off just as the train started rolling again.

We were miles from the Zhanjiang—miles from anywhere. In the parking lot a handful of women motorcycle taxi drivers stood with their bikes. One of them came over.

"Zhanjiang?" I asked again.

She looked at my piece of paper with the name of my hotel written in Chinese. She called another driver over. After some discussion, she nodded and held up five fingers. I wrote down 50 in my notebook (about $8), then showed it to her. She nodded and I knew it was too much, but I also knew that I was at her mercy, unless I wanted to spend the night in a rice paddy.

It took a long time to get to the hotel. My room had trees painted on the walls, colorful artwork, and a basket with a "Clean Towel for Trip (Inside Contain Gift)" and "99 Men Sex Oil," as well as a "Vibrating Ring Condom," all of which were "Non-Free" and seemed wise not to open.

Outside my window, the buildings of Zhanjiang were streaked with rust. This city was not listed in my guidebook, and for good reason: apart from a run-down amusement park on the waterfront, there was nothing to do. It had been a backwater for a long time. From 1898 through World War II, it was a French territory governed from afar and mostly left alone. All that was left of that time were a large church and a handful of crumbling French buildings.[134]

In the morning, I went downstairs and walked out into the street. There was a typhoon passing to the south, so the sky was dark and winds tore through the city. Trees bent sideways. Car alarms rang everywhere. A ship's horn echoed from the bay. Trash collectors pushed their carts up and down the road, bells clanging.

I walked up the main street, past the McDonald's and the Walmart, until I came to the Affiliated Hospital of Guangdong Medical College. The lobby was crowded with people all lined up to book appointments. Across the room, I saw an information desk. I walked over and showed the woman my piece of paper that said, *suo yang*. She pointed upstairs and wrote the number 3 on my paper. On the third floor, I came to a sign: BURN SURGERY, PAIN CLINIC, DRESSING ROOM AND UROLOGY.

The hall was dark and crowded. People milled in and out of the doctor's offices freely, the doors open. Finally I came to the room that said, UROLOGY. I poked my head in the door. The doctor turned. I reached into my pocket and took out my piece of paper.

"Do you ever see this?" I asked in English.

He took the paper, read it, shook his head slowly, then he looked at me.

"No," he said.

Outside, the wind had picked up. There were fewer people on the street. I walked down to the waterfront through the rain, then turned back to my hotel.

Late that night I woke up to the sound of someone yelling. It was still raining and the streets were empty except for one car that had stopped. In front of it a person was lying on the road. The driver paced back and forth, waving his arms, screaming.

I watched this for a long time. After an hour or so, an ambulance came and took everyone away. The car was still in the road, lights blinking. When I woke up the next morning, it was gone. And soon, not having found the old winds I sought, so was I.

9

STRANGE LOOPS

As I traveled south, closer to Hainan, closer to answers, I had a strong sense of moving through worlds that were held together by threads I couldn't see. Occasionally when I saw a temple or a church, my thoughts would drift back to another time when I'd had a similar feeling, not long after I returned from Italy.

My youngest brother had given up our family's boring old Methodism and converted to a new, vibrant, charismatic faith. He had visions of Jesus. He was alive in Christ. He was born again. He believed utterly—literally—in the bible. We, on the other hand, had been taught the whole thing was a vaguely historical metaphor.

I couldn't help but feel annoyed by his conversion. I was in the midst of struggling with my own beliefs, and I wasn't having much success with figuring things out. My brother, meanwhile, seemed genuinely happier: his life was starting to fall into place. What was more annoying was that he thought it would be equally good for the rest of us, so he'd invited me to come to his new church. I wanted to be a good brother and I was curious, so I agreed to go.

The Living Light services were held in an old Romanesque church on Winona's Main Street. The building had been constructed nearly a century ago, before it was sold off. Inside, all trappings of traditional Christianity were gone. At the front of the church, a woman playing the synthesizer warmed up in three chords and sang.

The pastor talked about God's hand in everything, about God's mysterious plan, about hell. He went on like this for what seemed like hours, and as he did, there was a tension building in his voice—an urgency that recalled both old tent revivals and new infomercials.

By the time the pastor mentioned speaking in tongues, I knew what was going to happen. You could feel it. People stood up and raised their palms. They rocked back and forth slightly until the spirit descended and they began rambling in a strange, rhythmic babble. I looked at my brother, who was also taken. How could we be so close, but be living in such different worlds?

Before that day, I'd always suspected speaking in tongues involved some fakery, some showmanship. But after that I knew I was wrong. What I saw was as real as the stones of the church. And what I took away from that day was the feeling that belief was the most powerful force at work in our lives, and that it could affect us at levels we hardly understood. To my brother, speaking in tongues was an indication of God's power. To me, it was an indication of our own.

Over the years when I've thought back to that day, I also wondered about my own beliefs. What were they? Where did I get them? What effects were they having on me?

I had seen my own brother believe something so strongly that it had caused him to speak in tongues, a phenomenon also known as "glossolalia."[135] Neuroscientists who study it have noticed spikes in the activity of some brain regions and drops in others. In this way his belief produced a physical reaction while I stood mute and unaffected because I didn't believe.

This was one of my first and clearest glimpses of how the

mind can exert its own raw power. My skepticism about the biomedical model deepened that day. What I saw was undeniably real. And if it was, then the mind couldn't be a passive byproduct of neurology. Once it emerged from the brain, it took on a reality of its own. Thinking about my brother in that church, I was confident that the flow between mind and brain—and mind and body—was more recursive than most of us assumed, and that our beliefs had some strong role to play.

No doubt this is why I was so fascinated by the culture-bound syndromes in the first place. They offered one of the clearest examples of this at work, of how beliefs shaped the contours along which our minds run, and of how those beliefs have powerful, tangible effects. Our beliefs, I felt sure, determined much about our lives that we didn't understand. Whereas in my brother's case his beliefs saved his life, the more I read about the syndromes, the more I began to see how in the wrong circumstances, your beliefs could also cost you your life.

This first came to my attention when I read Pow Meng Yap's 1951 paper, "Mental Diseases Peculiar to Certain Cultures." In it, he discusses the issue of "voodoo death," or "psychogenic death," or "thanatomania," where the belief that a person will die seems to cause their death.[136]

Yap was not the first person to investigate this. One of the early scientists who took it seriously was Walter Cannon, the pioneering doctor who first identified the "fight or flight" response. In 1942, Cannon wrote a paper titled "Voodoo Death," in which he gave examples from around the world of people dying from curses. This occurred in Lower Niger, the Congo, Brazil, New Zealand, and most notably in Australia, among the aborigines, where "bone pointing" had resulted in several well-documented deaths.[137]

Yet unlike his Western contemporaries, who thought these deaths were the product of overactive primitive minds, Cannon wasn't so quick to dismiss them as superstitious nonsense. He felt that the phenomenon was real—that it deserved further inquiry—and he proposed that the belief itself likely caused "persistent activity of the sympathico-adrenal system."[138]

From a strict biomedical perspective, voodoo death is impossible. How can what a person believes kill them? How can a curse cause someone's life to end? How can physical symptoms be caused by an idea? But Cannon knew that the mind and body were intertwined—that they were part of the same system, the same loop—and that each affected the other.

There were other instances of "voodoo death" scattered through the annals of medicine.[139] One of these occurred in 1967, when a young woman came into a Baltimore hospital complaining about shortness of breath, chest pains, nausea, and dizziness. She was two weeks short of her twenty-third birthday, and she hadn't had health problems until about a month earlier. She was extremely anxious. She was hyperventilating and sweating, and she nearly fainted. The doctor who admitted her reported she was obese, and thought she might be suffering from right-sided heart failure. Then, on her fourteenth day in the hospital, she finally told her doctor what her real problem was. As it turned out, she had only three days to solve it.

The woman had been born on Friday the 13th near Florida's Okefenokee Swamp. The midwife who delivered her and two other children that same day was a "rootworker" who told the girls' parents that all three children were hexed. The first girl would die before her sixteenth birthday. The second would die before her twenty-first. And the third—the woman in question—would die before she turned twenty-three.

As it happened, the first girl was killed in a car accident the day before her sixteenth birthday. The second girl made it to her twenty-first birthday and believed the spell was broken, so she went out to celebrate her good fortune. At the bar where she went, a fight broke out, a gun went off, and she was killed. This left the third woman convinced, beyond all doubt, that she would die as predicted. And the day before her twenty-third birthday, she did.[140]

How this works is not well understood—it is probably more complicated than what Cannon proposed. Yet you can see shades of it throughout our own culture in places far removed from the backwaters of the Okefenokee. In 1988, the journal *Advances in Biochemical Pharmacology* reported the case of a young man with AIDS whose mother found out he was gay on the same day that she was told about his disease. Disgusted, she set up a vigil outside his room, praying that he would die. The son could hear her prayers and he died an hour later, "much to the surprise of his physician, since he did not appear to be terminal."[141]

In 1974, a Tennessee man being treated for esophageal cancer was told his disease was fatal. He died two weeks later. But his autopsy found no cancer at all in his esophagus—just a few small nodes in his liver and one on his lung.[142] Nothing that should have killed him.

These are anecdotal, but there are other studies that point to the similar role belief may play in our demise. In the Framingham Heart Study, a massive multiyear study started in 1945 that continues through today, researchers found that women who believed they were at risk from heart disease were 3.6 times more likely to die of heart attacks than women with the same risk factors who believed they weren't.[143] Another study found that people who hold a negative view of aging die an average of 7.5 years before those with a positive view of it.[144] And in a survey of 28,169 Chinese Americans, David Phillips found that among victims of lymphatic cancer, those who were born in "earth years" (and who, according to traditional Chinese medicine, were more susceptible to "lumps, nodules, and tumors") died nearly four years before those who were born in other years. Those born in "metal years" with lung diseases like emphysema, asthma, and bronchitis (lungs are an "organ of metal") died five years earlier than those who had lung cancer but were *not* born in metal years. The size of the effect depended on "the strength of commitment to traditional Chinese culture."[145] Phillips also found a spike in deaths from cardiac arrest among Chinese and Japanese people on the fourth of every month. In those countries, the number 4 is considered unlucky.[146]

This all made a degree of sense to me, but how could it work? Was death—so extreme and final and physical—culture-bound, too? That seemed to be the implication of another strange episode that took place in the early 1980s among a group of people who were inexplicably dying in their sleep.

Not long after the first wave of Hmong immigrants began to arrive in the wake of the Vietnam War, reports began to emerge in the cities where they had settled that healthy young men were dying at night. They tended to be between twenty-five and forty-four years old, and had been in the United States for less than two years. Sometimes a relative would be awakened by the gasping and moaning only to watch helplessly as the victim died. Other times, they died alone. In total, 117 people were victims of what would be called "Sudden Unexpected Nocturnal Death Syndrome."[147]

American doctors looked everywhere for the cause—the victims' genes, their hearts, their metabolism, their mental health—but no mechanism could be found. The closest they came was an anomaly in the heart's electrical rhythms that seemed to be related to the deaths. But no one could say what caused this irregularity, or why it didn't kill others who had it. Eventually, it emerged that many of these young men had been repeatedly attacked in their sleep by a spirit called *dab tsog*, which comes in the night, sits on you, and keeps you from moving.

As Shelley Adler points out in *Sleep Paralysis: Night-mares, Nocebos, and the Mind-Body Connection*, her book about the phenomenon, these are the classic symptoms of the "nightmare," which has been common through world history. The ancient runic *mara* was a goblin that came and sat on your chest. In Newfoundland, it was known as the "old hag." In Italy, it was known as the *incubo*. In Germany, it was *Alpdruck* or "elf pressure." In China, it was *bei gui chaak*, or "being pressed by a ghost." Today in Western medicine, it's known as "sleep paralysis," and we believe it is a state when the mind has awakened but the body has not.[148]

Whatever you call it, it's utterly terrifying. I know this because once it happened to me. I was camping in the Badlands in South Dakota when I woke up with the feeling that two men were dragging me out of my tent. I couldn't move. There was a violent wind shaking the tarp. I saw the headlights of a car sweep across the campground. I tried to yell, but couldn't. Then slowly, I realized that my feet were facing the wrong side of the tent to actually be pulled out, and that this had to be some kind of dream. My heart was still pounding.

For me, this was an isolated incident—not part of any larger chain of events, any set of meanings. But in Hmong culture, there was a strong belief that your ancestors would protect you from evil spirits like the *dab tsog* as long as their graves were well-attended and the proper rituals were observed. But for the refugees in America, those graves were far away. Nearly a third of the Hmong population had been killed in the war, and another third had fled the ensuing genocide.

Yet even after coming to America, the belief remained strong. Adler found that 97 percent of Hmong immigrants she interviewed were familiar with *dab tsog*, and that 58 percent had had at least one attack.[149] In fact, when word spread of the nocturnal deaths, some men were so terrified they would set their alarm clocks to wake them up every twenty or thirty minutes.[150] They told Adler that if you were visited by the *dab tsog* once, or twice, and a Shaman couldn't help you, there was the possibility of an attack so bad you could die.[151]

They knew the danger. They knew the cause. They knew how the events would play out, deep in the night when they were lying on their backs alone, far from home.

Having been raised in a mechanistic culture, I still wanted to know exactly how this worked. How can death emerge from the psyche? How does belief actually kill? In her book, Adler suggests that SUNDS should be considered a version of the *nocebo effect*, the opposite of the *placebo effect*. While the Latin translation of placebo is "I will help," the translation of nocebo is, "I will harm."

For years now, there's been a growing body of research that challenges the idea that the body produces real effects and the mind does not. And where this is clearest is in research on the placebo and nocebo effects, a shift that began in 1978, when three researchers at the University of California San Francisco published a groundbreaking study. In it, patients who'd had impacted wisdom teeth removed were divided into two groups. After the operation, one group was given a placebo painkiller. Then (without their knowledge) they were given naloxone, an "opiate antagonist" that deactivates the opiates in your system. (Police spray it up the nose of people who've overdosed, and they are immediately revived.)

The second group was given one placebo painkiller, then another of the same.

Both groups felt a reduction in pain. But in the first group, pain began to rise after the naloxone had been given, even though the patients didn't know that they'd gotten it. Naloxone reduced the placebo effect, which showed that something more than imagination was at work. The belief that they were getting pain relief actually caused the patients' bodies to produce a painkiller.[152]

The study shook the medical field. It showed that the placebo response was more than a perception or a feeling. In the years since, many more studies have confirmed and expanded on those findings. The neuroscientist Fabrizio Benedetti has found that painkillers given surreptitiously are far less effective than those given in full view: It takes much higher dosages of a hidden painkiller to get the same relief. Similarly, he found the anxiety drug diazepam worked much better when given with the patient's knowledge than when given secretly (in which case it didn't work at all). And he also showed how patients with Parkinson's needed nearly twice the voltage of deep brain stimulus when the treatment was hidden from them to get the same effect as when they knew what to expect.[153]

Why is this? Benedetti and others believe we have a kind of evolved internal healthcare system that can be activated by a healer and the healing ritual,[154] and that many of our modern drugs are effective because they use pathways that are already there. That's why when a patient with migraines takes either a placebo labeled as the drug Maxalt or the drug Maxalt labeled as a placebo, the pain relief they receive is nearly equal.

But when they take Maxalt correctly labeled as Maxalt, the effect is more than twice as big: the drug combined with the belief in its efficacy works better than either alone.[155]

I was excited to read about this research. Here was more proof that the mind must be a participant in the biological process—that the two weren't wholly separate. And while the parameters of the placebo and nocebo effects haven't been fully mapped yet, it has been shown to be active in the immune system, the circulatory system, and various brain regions. In a study of people who needed arthroscopic knee surgery, those who received placebo surgery (a few cuts to make it look like surgery) had the same level of improvement one to two years later as those who got the real surgery.[156]

Similar experiments have been done on people who've had surgery for angina pectoris, pacemakers, and, most recently, a back surgery called vertebroplasty, which some 750,000 people in the United States get each year, and which generates somewhere between $12 and $18 billion in annual medical expenses.[157] In one study, vertebroplasty and placebo groups had pain ratings of 6.9 and 7.2 before the procedure and 3.9 and 4.6 a month later respectively, a difference that was "neither statistically significant nor clinically meaningful." This doesn't mean the surgery didn't help. But it does mean the reason it helped wasn't the surgery itself.[158]

This works the opposite way too. The nocebo response uses different mechanisms, but the effect is the same. In a randomized controlled trial of 270 people with chronic arm pain, patients were given either a placebo pill or sham acupuncture, in which the needle doesn't actually penetrate the skin. Before the study, the patients were warned about side effects, and 31 percent of the pill group and 25 percent of the acupuncture group experienced precisely the side effects they'd been warned about.[159] Three people even dropped out of the study because their fatigue or dry mouth were so severe.[160]

Other studies have shown similar outcomes. When volunteers were told that a mild electrical current being passed through their heads could give them a headache, two-thirds got headaches, even though there was no current.[161] In a study of lactose intolerance, participants were given glucose and told it was lactose. Afterward, 44 percent of those with lactose intolerance developed stomach symptoms.[162] In one experiment in the 1960s, patients given sugar water were told it would make them vomit, and 80 percent of them did just that.[163]

In other words, as the anthropologist Daniel Moerman has written in his book *Meaning, Medicine and the "Placebo Effect,"* "there is more to biology than biology."[164] Moerman argues that it is the *meaning* of their treatment that activates these effects. For Benedetti, the key is a person's *expectation* of what will happen, or the conditioning he or she has received from prior treatments.[165]

But to me, the word that encompasses both these interpretations is belief: belief in the surgery, belief in the surgeon, belief in biochemistry, belief in the power of the pill, belief that one thing will cause another to happen, and belief that a certain medicine or operation will have a certain effect.[166]

I came across one more study Moerman cited that showed even more clearly how such belief can flow from person to person, from doctor to patient, and from a patient's mind to his or her own body.

In a double blind study on doctors *and* patients, there were two groups of clinicians. The first group was told their patients would either receive naloxone (which would increase their pain), an inert pill (a placebo) or fentanyl (a painkiller 80 times more powerful than morphine). The second group of doctors was told

that the fentanyl was being held up by an administrative problem, so the patient would only get either naloxone or a placebo.

In the first group (patients who got a placebo from doctors who thought their patients might get fentanyl), pain
decreased by two points one hour after treatment. In the
second (patients who got a placebo from doctors who *didn't*
believe they would be administering fentanyl), pain increased
by six points. What they got and what they were told were the
same. Only who they got it from had changed.[167]

In a given culture, we believe all kinds of things. We
believe in magic or God or karma or biochemistry, and we
don't really know what effects those beliefs might be having
on us or how they might interact with our biology.

In our culture, for example, we've long believed that
stress is damaging and should be avoided at all costs. But in
her book *The Upside of Stress*, Kelly McGonigal shows that
it is actually our belief in this fact that does the harm. In a
study of nearly 28,000 Americans conducted over eight years,
high levels of stress increased risk of death by 43 percent—but
only for people who believed stress was harmful. People who
had stress but didn't believe in its harmfulness actually lived
the longest of any group surveyed.[168] It seems that our belief
about the nature of an experience can change the way our
bodies respond to it. What McGonigal calls our "mindset"[169]
acts as a kind of gatekeeper for our physiological reactions to
the things we do and experience.[170]

Your mind changes your body's response.

People who believe stress is harmful have what's called
"threat response." Their blood flow restricts, their hearts beat
faster, their inflammation and immune function ramp up—
all in anticipation of potential injury. People who don't believe
stress is harmful have a "challenge response," in which blood

flow remains strong, blood vessels are relaxed, and the heart beats with more force (not just more speed).[171] They also tend to have higher levels of the stress hormone DHEA, which is associated with a lower risk of depression, anxiety, heart disease, and other things we'd like to avoid.[172]

To me, this sounded so much like the cultural syndromes that it seemed like you could make the case that our stress response was a kind of cultural syndrome itself—a damaging cycle caused in part by our beliefs. This wasn't mind over matter. It was mind *and* matter. It was the mind interpreting and then altering the matter. If the mind—the person we feel we are—emerges from the brain, then here was a kind of feedback loop where that mind turns around to change the brain it emerged from.

On a gut level, this seems impossible. But it's been revealed again and again. For example, the social psychologist Amy Cuddy and her colleagues have found that your body posture can actually change testosterone levels.[173] And the neuroscientist Richard Davidson and his colleagues have revealed how meditation can alter which genes are activated or dormant in a way that "may have a substantive impact on biological processes critical for physical health."[174]

So how exactly are mental and physical health intertwined? That's the question Western medicine had been struggling with. In much of modern neuroscience, biomedical dogma still reigns. We expect neurological explanations for everything, and we look to neuroscientists as a kind of priesthood that can explain who we are and how we got that way. This is what's known as upward causation: the belief that everything about us can be explained on a biochemical level.

But there are a few dissenting voices, including that of neuroscientist Michael Gazzaniga, who holds that "top-down causation" from the mental back to the physical is possible, and that our mental states do affect our physical states.[175] The mind, in other words, is not reducible to the brain. It is more than the sum of its parts—or at least different from them— and it can change (within limits) the way those parts work.

This was what I had seen in my brother's church: the mind—and belief—causing changes in the brain. And it's what I later saw in Nigeria: fear and belief creating the real sensation that the penis was gone. And this, almost certainly, was the missing piece in the mysterious Hmong deaths. While researchers looked everywhere for a physical cause, the missing piece was in the mind, in the victims' beliefs, and in the way their minds and their bodies interacted.

In his book *Mad Travelers: Reflections on the Reality of Transient Mental Illnesses*, the philosopher Ian Hacking has written about illnesses that appear at certain points of time and then, oddly, fade away. One example is *fugue*. In the late 1800s, *fugue* was all the rage. It had begun with a man named Albert Dadas, who lived in Bordeaux, France, and who had an uncontrollable compulsion to travel. When he was twelve years old he disappeared from his home in Bordeaux. A neighbor told his father they'd seen him walking toward the coast, and his brother found him in the city of La Teste, with no idea how he'd gotten there.

Dadas's disassociated journeys got farther and farther from home. He was "tormented with the need to travel." He went as far as Algiers, Berlin, Budapest, and Moscow, where he was arrested while admiring a statue of Peter the Great, because police thought he was a nihilist. In 1887 he was diagnosed with *fugue*.

"Medical reports of Albert set off a small epidemic of compulsive mad voyagers whose epicenter was Bordeaux, but which soon spread to Paris, all France, Italy, and, later, Germany and Russia," writes Hacking. "Fugue became a medical disorder in its own right," with names like *Wandertrieb* in Germany and *automatisme ambulatoire, determiniso ambulatorio,* and *poriomanie* in other places.[176]

And yet, *fugue* soon all but disappeared. It had sounded so official, so medical, so biological. And then it was gone. Hacking argues that history is in fact full of conditions like this, which are de rigueur for a time, but which vanish when people no longer believe in the ideas behind them. He cites hysteria and multiple personality disorder as two examples of transient disorders where certain beliefs (both by society and the person) are part of the cause. Other possible candidates include chronic fatigue syndrome, anorexia, bulimia, and intermittent explosive disorder.

No matter what you put on a list like this, a debate inevitably unspools over what is biological and what is psychological, what is real and what is not. "Transient mental illnesses," Hacking writes, "provoke banal debates about whether they are 'real' or 'socially constructed.' We need richer tools with which to think than reality or social construction."[177]

Hacking suggests that *fugue* and other conditions can flourish in a place and time because the right conditions exist in the same way that ecological conditions allow certain species to arise—the kiwi, the giant sloth, the snail darter. When those conditions change, the animals die out. In the late 1800s, a niche opened up in Europe to allow *fugue* to arise, and then it was gone.[178] As a kind of resolution of the dichotomy, Hacking has proposed the term "bioloop" to describe the process by which our ideas and beliefs affect our physiology, and our physiology in turn affects our minds.[179]

Devon Hinton is a cultural psychiatrist who studies a

cultural syndrome called "*khyâl* attacks" among Cambodian patients. This is where the flow of *khyâl* (something like wind) through the body reverses course, causing coldness in the hands, a feeling that one's neck vessels are going to explode, and occasionally makes victims collapse to the floor unable to speak or move.

Hinton says *khyâl* attacks are related to the biology of anxiety and panic, but the "cultural frame" causes them to have radically different symptoms than those of people who have panic attacks in our culture. He and his fellow researchers call this "bioattentional looping,"[180] where your fear causes you to survey your body for symptoms, which you find, which then increase your fear and so on, in a vicious cycle.

"There's no doubt that the cultural frames are driving it in part, but to what extent we don't know," Hinton told me.

The idea of a bioloop is the most elegant solution: the notion that there is a kind of circle of causation, that mental and physical states are connected so that each alters the other to some degree. A biolooping effect doesn't imply that one is real and one is not. It doesn't imply that biology doesn't matter or that drugs don't work. It doesn't mean that thoughts are magical or that we can believe anything we want and then produce it. It doesn't even imply that any of these things are easily divided into different categories. Rather, they are all part of the same tangled organism. Cultural syndromes—and all syndromes—are a result of these loops. Each of us exists in a swirl of belief and expectancy and biology. Each of us is a very strange loop.

One day in Minneapolis I met a young Hmong woman named Sandy'Ci Moua, who'd been featured in a local news

story about a new generation of Hmong shamans.[181] Moua
was born in Minnesota, but grew up surrounded by Hmong
language and culture; when she first got to college, she would
eat the food off her white friends' plates because she thought
everyone ate family style. She is a performance artist and
works for the city of Brooklyn Park as a community liaison.

Moua went to a Christian church for years. But whenever
she found herself at a Hmong funeral home, she would see
spirits and talk to them. Other times, she would see deceased
people. Her family had a history of mental illness, but that
same family included a long line of shamans: both men and
women. So she started pursuing that path, only to leave it for
complicated reasons (including the realization, as she put it,
that shamanism was based more in fear than love). When I
met her, she called herself "spiritually homeless." I told her I
wanted to know if people today still saw the *dab tsog* at night.

"Everyone has heard stories," she says. "They want to
know, 'What happens? What do you do?' It happened to
me once. You just turn on your side really quick. There is a
Hmong Ghost Story page on Facebook. They talk about it
incessantly."

"And does it still kill people?" I asked.

"I don't think so. I haven't heard about it. But I don't
really ask that many questions about it."

We talked about many things, about how much had
changed for the Hmong people in their forty years in America, about how Moua switches codes when talking to young
and old people in the Hmong community.

"The luxury for the third generation," Moua said, "is that
they can just be themselves all the time, and not worry about
what they are, and what they wear. They have the ability to
shape their own narrative more, and not feel the pressure to

judge it or qualify it as this or that. When I was growing up, I was called 'whitewashed' and I was called 'fresh off the boat' at the same time! Two completely opposite insults. But I don't think they say that much anymore."

Moua told me she worries that when the older generation dies, they will take many things with them, like the traditional wedding rituals, with their intricate, lyrical language.

"I try to tell myself that it's not helpful for me to have anxiety about it. I'm just going to ride the wave. Old cultures die and new cultures emerge. That's the way life is. I can't control it. It's not up to me. But I wish there was a book that said, 'When in doubt, go to page five.'

"But there is no book. We're not a text-based culture. We learn through stories. We just absorb it. But we don't know all the words. We don't know what to do. And if we don't know it, we can't be bound by it."

My brother and I never talked about speaking in tongues. Though that day in church had a huge impact on me, I nonetheless remained unconverted, so it was never mentioned again. We retreated into our separate worlds and traveled in different directions. But now, years later, we've arrived a place where we're more at ease with each other's beliefs, many of which have been tempered by age.

One day I called him to ask about those times, and it turned out that he was happy to talk about it. He remembered Living Light Church well and recalled speaking in tongues there many times. It was a powerful experience for him, coming from the Methodist tradition, which was dusty and boring and abstract. At the new church, there was God—tangible, alive, and undeniably true.

But as time went on, he went to other churches with other traditions and other understandings, and he saw people speak in tongues in other ways. Some were a kind of babble; others sounded like an actual language. He met Christians who saw speaking in tongues as something that belonged in the first century AD, and others who thought it the work of the devil. He even met people who used its powers in ways they shouldn't.

Today he doesn't doubt the reality of speaking in tongues or the power of the gift. "It is very relaxing," he told me, when I asked how it felt. "It's like you're putting yourself into a mindset where you're receiving somebody else's input and just kind of processing that. That's kind of the way I view it. I can't do this if I'm in the way."

But his thoughts on it are more complex than they once were. He can see now how the experience depends not solely on God, but on other factors: on your maturity level, on your life experience, on your understanding of what exactly is being given. The gift may be real, but the person plays a certain part in deciding what it sounds like, what it means, and what it is.

These days, he doesn't speak in tongues much anymore. He and his family go to a church where people don't do it during the service, though some might in private. And on the whole, it just isn't as important to him as it used to be.

"When I was young," he said, "what was important to me was truth. What I didn't read was that Jesus was full of truth *and* grace. Because when it comes down to it, he said, 'Love your neighbor as yourself.' He didn't say, 'Go speak in tongues.'"

Whereas once he believed that the gift of tongues was the point of it all, he now sees that it was a more like a sign along the road to some other place. What once felt like the end of his story turned out to be the beginning.

10

THE DRAGON'S TAIL

In my mind, I'd pictured the city of Haikou as an island town with palm trees and grass huts and people lounging under them. But as the ferry got closer. I could see this was not the case. Haikou, the capital city of Hainan Island, looked more like Miami, with beachfront high-rises stretching as far as I could see.

We all climbed off the boat at the port, into a sea of cab drivers. I got on a motorcycle taxi and showed the driver a piece of paper with the Twinkle Star Youth Hostel on it. We were off.

Once I arrived, I checked in (which took nearly an hour using Google Translate), threw my bags into my room, then walked back down to where the hostel workers and their friends sat around a table playing a drinking game with cards stuck to their foreheads. They asked me to join them, so I did.

None of them, it turned out, was from Hainan. The island felt like it was a long way from anywhere in China. Historically, it was known for its pearls and jade, its opium and pirates. It was often referred to as the "tail of the dragon," and for hundreds of years it remained a place most Chinese people could barely imagine. It lay beyond the dreaded "Gate of Ghosts" and served as the place of ultimate exile for unwanted political figures. Passage from the mainland to the island "marked a sort of spiritual death," according to the historian Edward Schafer.[182] The poet and politician Su Dongpo was once sent to Hainan by the Emperor in 1094 AD, in part for his poetry:

> *Families when a child is born*
> *Hope it will turn out intelligent.*
> *I, through intelligence*
> *Having wrecked my whole life,*
> *Only hope that the baby will prove*
> *Ignorant and stupid.*
> *Then he'll be happy all his days*
> *And grow into a Cabinet Minister.*[183]

Hainan was barely seen as part of China. There were no roads to the interior until the 1950s. In the early twentieth century, the father of modern China, Sun Yat-sen (whose wife's family was Hainanese) tried to sell the island for $14 million.[184]

No one would dream of doing that today. Hainan is booming. The sky over Haikou is so full of construction cranes that it looks like Dubai circa 2005. People are flooding in from across China, and at long last there is talk of building a bridge to the mainland.

After a couple rounds of the drinking game, I called a woman I'd been e-mailing named Marian Rosenberg. It was late at night, but we decided to meet for a beer anyway. Marian was from Baltimore. She was loud and brash and not shy about voicing her opinions. She owned the Haikou #1 Translation Agency and had piles of work translating brochures for local golf resorts and other businesses. She genuinely loved Hainan—her feelings toward it were warmer than those of Su Dongpo, who had described it this way:

The climate of Hainan is damp
and a humid swampy atmosphere
rises from the ground rotting everything
How can a human being stand it for so long?[185]

Marian could stand it. It helped that every year or so, she would pack her things and bike across China on various 2,000-mile routes before returning to the swampy atmosphere, where rambutan and Southeast Asian fruit were plentiful.

I told Marian that I wanted to go to Lin'gao,[186] where the 1984 *koro* epidemic started. On paper, this seemed simple enough, as it was only about fifty miles from Haikou. Before arriving, I figured it wouldn't involve much more than a bus ride and a translator.

But the way Marian paused made me think this would be more complicated. As she explained, even though Lin'gao was less than an hour's drive from Haikou, it was still a world away.

Hainan is not like the rest of China. The official language is Mandarin and the common tongue is Hainanese, but there are at least ten other languages spoken on the Island. None of these are mutually intelligible.[187] In other words, each town had its own language, its own history, its own traditions, and its own culture. When the researchers had come from Guangzhou to investigate the *suo yang* epidemic, to some villagers they would have seemed almost as foreign as me.

Marian said that she would try to find a translator who spoke Lin'gaohua, a cousin of Thai, and the language spoken in Lin'gao.

For the next several days, I tried to amuse myself in Haikou. This was not easy. Haikou is not a tourist town.[188] It's a town where Chinese people come to make money or to escape the crush of the rest of the country. There were no maps of the city in English and there weren't any signs I could read. I had to find my way around by looking at the angles of the streets and trying to match them up to a Chinese map I bought in a shop.

Luckily, Marian lent me her bike share card, so I was able to ride the rickety red one-speeds locked at various kiosks around the city. That was how I got to the Hainan Museum, a large, austere, temple-like building on the other side of town.

The museum was full of dioramas, some of which had been translated. One informed me: "In ancient times, [Hainan] was regarded as an island, savage and wild with waste and miasma, communicable subtropical diseases." The religions of Hainan were listed as: Buddhism, Islamism, Taoism, Christianism, Primitive Religions and Matsu Worship, "a goddess embraced by boatman, sailors, passengers, merchants and fisherfolks."

One display said that in 110 BC, a Han Dynasty's general landed his army here, and "Han culture took roots in the hearts of the people, with its broad, profound, gentle and positive characters and gradually became the mainstream of Hainan culture."

But another read: "Later on, the aboriginals resisted against the governing of the central government and the two [established] counties were forced to be dismissed from the office for nearly one hundred years." By 42 AD, the central government had "calmed down the rebellion."

According to the reports published by the Guangzhou Brain Hospital, the *suo yang* epidemic started in Lin'gao in August 1984, when a fortune teller "predicted that 1985 would be a bad year and that all of the people would suffer from many disasters."[189]

After that, rumors spread of a fox ghost—sometimes disguised an old woman roaming the land—collecting penises in covered baskets she carried on a shoulder pole.[190] When two young men approached her and told her to uncover the baskets, they looked inside, saw that the baskets were filled with penises and died instantly of fright.

Panic about *koro* would hit a village and last three to four days. When residents heard about a case in a neighboring village, the panic would subside, since that meant the ghost had moved on. The attacks slowly made their way around the island. The ghost struck at night, when villagers were sleeping. A chill would creep into the room, and suddenly the victim would feel his penis shrinking inward. He would grab it and run outside for help. A twenty-eight-year-old office worker was at home one night when

> he heard a gong being beaten and the terrifying noises made by people who were panicking in a nearby neighborhood. He suddenly became anxious and experienced the sensation that his penis was shrinking. He was seized with panic and shouted loudly for help. Several men in the neighborhood rushed in and tried to rescue him by forcefully pulling his penis and making loud sounds to chase away the evil ghost that was thought to be affecting him.[191]

Neighbors and family members were enlisted in rescue operations. Victims were beaten with sandals and slippers while the middle finger of their left had was squeezed, so that the ghost could exit the body there.[192]

The epidemic engulfed the island, with the exception of the Li and Miao minorities, who seemed to be immune to such fears. Researchers estimated that between 2,000 and 5,000 people were affected,[193] but that "no one died from genital retraction."[194] One baby, however, did die when his mother tried to feed him pepper juice, and a girl was beaten to death during a two-hour exorcism.

"Numerous men suffered injuries to their penises as a result of 'rescuing' actions."[195] Iron pins were sometimes inserted through the nipples of women to prevent retraction, which caused infections as well.

Afterward, researchers found that 100 percent of victims had prior knowledge of *suo yang*, and 100 percent had a fear of death due to genital retractions. After all, this had happened in Hainan before and people knew the stories. Older residents "vividly remembered episodes of epidemics in 1948, 1955, 1966 and 1974" that affected hundreds.[196] In the end, researchers concluded that *koro* was a "culture-related psychiatric disorder," since the traditional beliefs made it, "'possible,' 'familiar' and 'real,'" to the islanders.[197]

Which is exactly how stories work: First they make things possible. Then they make them familiar. Then they make them real. The difference between victims and non-victims was that they knew exactly what to expect.

One afternoon, I went over to the University Hospital with a young women named Sansa Wang, who worked as Marian's assistant and who spoke excellent English. She was also from the north and had come to study at the university in Haikou, a city that she didn't want to leave. Together we rode the elevator up to the office of a certain Dr. Wang (no relation to Sansa). He practiced Chinese Medicine at the hospital.

Dr. Wang looked slightly worn down by things—or maybe by us. He leaned over his desk, hands folded in front of him. But he was polite, and answered my questions as best as he could. Sansa explained what I was looking for.

"I've heard of *suo yang*," he said, "but I've never seen such patients."

"Do some people still panic about it?" I asked.

"People panic about this less now than some years ago." Dr. Wang said.

"So the belief is less strong?"

"Yes."

"But it still happens?"

"In history there were two periods when this happened on a large scale. One was in the 1980s. The other was in a village, and about ten or twelve people got it, and they felt panicked and after that happened they went to the doctor."

"And when was that?"

"Maybe three years ago, in Sanya."

We thanked him, then left. Sanya was a city on the south end of Hainan Island. Maybe *koro* was still here, still alive.

Marian suggested I meet her doctor, Cassie Zhou, who'd been educated in Oklahoma, and who was a strict believer in Western medicine. She didn't fear bad winds, didn't believe in hot or cold. She talked about cells and circulation and biochemistry. I was more curious to know how the world in which she was educated blended with the one in which she practiced. How could you possibly integrate the two?

We met at a restaurant not far from the hospital. It was loud, and the décor was bright red. Dr. Cassie had never heard of *koro*, and no patients had ever come into her office with it.

"In China," she said, "most doctors' training is in Western medicine. But even the Chinese medicine doctors, they also use Western medicine. So sometimes it's a combination of both. The difficulty is that sometimes we don't know which one is really working. If people just take Chinese medicine, and say, 'Oh, this medicine works,' actually it might be the placebo, and not really the Chinese medicine."

She went on to talk about the generational difference she saw.

"When I talk to older patients," she said, "I have to explain things using terms like fire, and yin and yang, and wind. In general, the younger generation are well educated, and so more specific information is better. But the older ones, they always ask me questions like, 'I'm too hot, and I have too much fire in my body and you need to give me some medicine to put down the fire.' It's hard to explain to them, 'I don't believe there's a fire.' Because they might have diabetes and feel dizzy and feel that their yin is too low. I think at least half my patients believe that. It's such a cultural thing."

Zhou struggled with the fact that after giving birth, women refused to leave the house for one month due to fear of wind.

"They feel that when you have a baby, your whole body is open, and your womb is opened up. So if you are exposed to the wind, and the wind is coming into your body, you will be sick for the rest of your life. There is a culture of this in China. And they have to have many layers of clothes, and they're not allowed to wash their hair or brush their teeth.

"That happens today?" I asked.

"Yes, even today. Even for doctors. All over China. Almost everybody. It's so hard. What I explain to them is that I had two children, and I didn't do that and I don't think that's true.

So some of them might compromise a little with the culture, and say, 'Okay, I will wash my hair or brush my teeth, but I will not go outside or have the windows open.' They're afraid this could be a curse for the rest of their lives. Even my nurse talked about this all the time when she had a baby."

"Is there any difference between local Hainanese and mainlanders?"

"The local people believe that when you are sick you should not eat eggs or chicken or fish. So my patients always ask me, when they are sick, 'What can I eat or not eat?' I say, 'Whatever you like to eat.'"

That afternoon, I went back to the Twinkle Star and sat on the roof. The wind was strong and light rain fell. Later that night, Marian called with good news. She had found a person in Lin'gao who spoke English and Mandarin. His name was Dennis.

11

THE CHAINS THAT BIND US

As the sun set on Hainan, I sat and tried to write in my journal, but kept getting distracted by the dogs barking and running around the construction site across the street. The rain stopped, but the wind from the typhoon still blew as it moved out of the area, after destroying crops and lives across the island.

I wrote some more, then set my pen down and let my thoughts go back to the questions that had brought me this far, including the one that had gnawed at me for years: If our beliefs were so powerful, such a key piece of the bioloop, then where did they come from? How do we get them from the people around us? How do they become part of us? How do we pass them on?

The wind was a powerful force in southern China. It felt almost supernatural, and I could see why stories would arise about it, how powers could be attributed to it.[198] Some ancient Chinese medical texts cautioned against "wind insanity" and "wind stupidity."[199] Even today, as I'd just heard, new mothers were deathly afraid of it.

To the north in the village of Fuhu, the old woman blamed an "evil wind" for the 2004 outbreak. Yet all the boys who'd been afflicted with *suo yang* (with the exception of the first one) suffered attacks *after* they'd heard the story from their headmaster. Since they trusted their headmaster and knew the student, they began to feel the effects of the story as it made its way into their body, by way of their minds, as the story began to take on a reality of its own. To me, it seemed like a different wind was at work.

Hearing about a cultural syndrome was one of the primary risk factors. The same pattern could be seen in the Hainan and Singapore epidemics. All the victims first learned about it happening to others. It was the same pattern in the Indian city of Bikaner, where people suffered from gilhari (lizard) syndrome. In Bikaner, 928 of 1,000 people surveyed had heard about it, whereas in nearby Jaipur and Delhi, where there was no such syndrome, not a single person had heard of such a thing. Either the lizard didn't live there, or the stories didn't.

Stories are something I always understood. I didn't grow up in a storytelling family. My father tells what he likes to think are stories, but they're more like sequential chains of loosely connected factual events. My mother keeps a three-line diary in which she catalogs the day's events, which is more like the raw material from which stories are made.

In Bridgit's family, however, there are a number of easy raconteurs who tell stories roughly based on things that happened, but with deep feelings at their core. Her father, for example, likes to tell a story about how Bridgit's first car was a huge Lincoln Continental that was so big she could barely see over the dashboard—he could barely see her head when she was in it. He got her that car, he says, because he wanted to make sure she was surrounded by as much steel as possible.

Except that wasn't it exactly. The Lincoln was just one of several cars her family owned and that she drove. Another was a tiny Datsun that would have been smashed like a tin can if it had hit another vehicle. Her first car was actually a rusted Ford Tempo.

For a long time I puzzled over this discrepancy. It took me years to finally understand that this wasn't really a story about her first car. It was a story about how much he loved his daughter and wanted her to be protected from the world. All that steel was his love.

So what makes a story into a story? There are platitudes that everyone seems to agree with: storytelling is a human universal,[200] we've been sharing stories for most of our time on earth, and on and on. But how exactly could we define the difference between, say, a story and a chronological ledger? What makes one telling a story and another a collection of facts?

For a long time I looked for an answer to this question, until I finally stumbled across it in a field about as far from the English department as you can get: artificial intelligence.

Computer programs, it turns out, cannot understand stories. This is one of the biggest problems with creating intelligence. What's at issue is something called "commonsense causal reasoning," which means understanding instantly when one thing causes another to happen. It's something we do naturally, effortlessly.

I spoke with Andrew Gordon, a researcher at the University of Southern California's Institute for Creative Technologies who has been working on this problem for years.

"It's very simple things," he told me. "Like if you tell the computer you dropped an egg, you want the computer to know that it broke, not bounced."[201]

Gordon and his fellow researchers tried to recreate this ability by collecting millions of stories from blogs and using them to teach the computer how to see that A causes B. After they collected these stories, they designed a test to ask it questions like: "The man lost his balance on the ladder. What happened as a result? 1: He fell off the ladder. 2: He climbed up the ladder." Or: "The man fell unconscious. What was the cause of this? 1: The assailant struck the man in the head. 2: The assailant took the man's wallet."

Computers are horrible at this test, whereas humans get the answer right 99 percent of the time—more or less perfectly. Using the millions of stories from the internet, the best result Gordon and his colleagues could get from the computer was 65 percent, or just 15 percent better than pure chance.[202] For a computer, a Lincoln Continental is just a car. Steel is just steel.

"There's not a culture that doesn't tell stories," Gordon said. "It's something embedded in our genes that makes us good storytellers. It's a huge survival advantage, because you can encapsulate important information from one person to another and share it within a group. So there's a good reason to be good storytellers."

The historian Yuval Harari argues that between 70,000 and 30,000 years ago, humans underwent a "Cognitive Revolution," that let us surpass (or defeat) other human-like creatures. It did this by allowing us to imagine stories about the world around us—to create the legends, myths, gods, and religions that helped us work together, as groups, toward imagined goals.[203]

This was certainly a leap. But the roots of this ability were older, more fundamental. The heart of storytelling's usefulness is the way it conveys causality. The fall causes the egg to break. The wobbling causes the man to fall. When you tell a story, you're trying to bring what Gordon calls "causal coherence" to events that are separated by time.[204] In other words, it's not just that they happened in order, one before the other. It's that they are connected, that one causes the other to happen.

Whether computers will ever be able to understand both

what happens in a story and why it happened (as well as why that matters) remains uncertain, but Gordon feels he's getting closer, that it's only a matter of time before machines can run causal chains forward and backward in time.[205]

We, on the other hand, are already there and have been for tens of thousands of years. We see causality constantly, incessantly, and effortlessly. We see it when we read the news, or when we talk about our neighbors, or when we watch a movie or read a book. It is always the first question in our mind when we see an accident on the highway, or hear of a spectacular crime, or learn of an old friend who ended badly: What caused this?

One of the first people to notice this was a Belgian scientist named Albert Michotte, who studied the psychology of perception in the early 1900s. Michotte had doctorates in both philosophy and physiology, and he wanted to break down human behavior into smaller units the way biology was breaking the human body down into cells and nerves. For him, perception was the smallest unit of all.[206]

In his laboratory, Michotte showed people images of a rectangle that would move across their field of vision and then stop next to another one, which proceeded to move off at a slower speed. At certain speeds, he found, subjects always saw the first rectangle as *causing* the second to move. This and other experiments led him to conclude that the perception of causality was instinctive, automatic, even sensory, the same way we smell or hear or see. He noted that our ability to see causality around us can appear as early as age four.[207] But today we know it can be detected in infants as well. We do not learn it. We know it almost from the day we are born.

Another thing that struck Michotte was how people would see the shapes as quarrelling or hunting or being afraid of each other, when in fact they were just shapes and were doing none of these things. People couldn't help seeing causality. They looked at shapes and saw stories.[208]

In 1944, a pair of researchers named Fritz Heider and Marianne Simmel built on this insight. They created an animation in which a small triangle, a big triangle, and a circle interacted around a square.[209] Watching the shapes move around one another, it was impossible for people not to see a kind of story where the big triangle bullied the little one, or where the circle and small triangle banded together, or some other version where the shapes had motives that caused them to act from the inside. People saw fear and anger and cooperation. Without these, there was no story. There were just lines on a page.

As with shapes, so with life. We look around us and see causal links—motives and meaning. We do not see randomness, as Albert Camus once argued.[210] We see stories. We see love and hate, strength and weakness, goodness and badness causing people to act the way they do. We see luck and magic, God and ghosts, fate and physics pushing the pieces of the world around us. Every story contains its own answer to the question "Why?" And the stories we tell about these things follow paths we recognize, paths as old as humankind, paths to redemption, to contamination, to heroism, to tragedy, to comedy.

The neuroscientist Michael Gazzaniga studies the difference between the brain's hemispheres and he has found: "It is the left hemisphere that engages in the human tendency to find order in chaos, that tries to fit everything into a story and put it into a context."[211] Gazzaniga calls this side the "interpreter."[212] But perhaps the left hemisphere should really be called the "storyteller," because it helps us see everything that slides beneath our stories' surfaces. These are the things that hold our stories together—the things that we believe in.

One of the reasons for my many failures as a young writer was that I thought that stories were just interesting things that happened. I thought I could write about these interesting things and people would read what I wrote. The problem was that I didn't know what they meant or why they mattered. I had no idea what the causal links were, either within the story itself or to the larger world.

That's what I tell myself. That's what I believe when I look back on my failures, on the way I could tell you everything about Bruno Manser except what his life meant—or meant to me—if it meant anything at all, which maybe it didn't. But now it does. Now it has become part of my "life story," which is something we all have.

Stories are not just how we stitch the world together. They are how we stitch our selves together. Our life is literally a story that we tell ourselves,[213] and building that life story is a process that begins around the time we turn two years old. That's when we develop what the psychologist Dan McAdams calls a "primitive autobiographical self." As we move into adolescence, we start to emphasize different memories we feel were important—events from which we learned something or changed. Then during our late teens we start to develop a more complicated "personal fable" in which we dream of the people we might one day become, like astronauts and presidents. McAdams calls this a "first draft" of our identity. We choose episodes based not only on who we think we are, but also on who we hope to be.[214]

As we move into young adulthood (between ages seventeen and twenty-five), we try to compose a "full life story" that explains not only how we got to where we are, but also what we believe, and who we will actually end up being.

Unless we write a memoir or visit a therapist, we may never share this life story with anyone. But that doesn't make it any less important. McAdams and others argue that the ability to see one's life as a story is at the heart of identity. In fact, our ability to "narrate" our life's events may even be the defining mark of consciousness.

For most of us, our full life story is never really finished and is always subject to revision.[215] Even so, it determines much of how our life unfolds. It's like a road map through the chaos with arrows pointing one way or another at turning points like failure and success, death and birth, love and loss.

During the years I spent trying and failing to write about places like Tanzania, Thailand, and Borneo, my own life story was fragmented, patched together, ad hoc, and not ready for public consumption. But still it was important to work on it, to think about it, to edit it, to revise it, and to add new chapters. Because the power of the life story—even the power of *thinking* about it—has effects that can be detected throughout our lives, and even in our biology.

This was something the psychologist Jamie Pennebaker discovered in the early 1980s. For years he'd been interested in the relationship between the mental and the physical, in the way they interact, and how "psychological conflicts are linked to specific changes in our bodies,"[216] as he writes in his book *Opening Up*.

Pennebaker's interest stemmed from his own experience. As a child growing up in dusty western Texas, he'd had asthma every winter. After he left home, he never had it again, except when he went home for Christmas. But in his last year of college, his parents came to visit and he had an asthma attack, which suggested that his asthma wasn't entirely a result of particles in the air, but also of something in his mind, something connected to his own conflicts with his parents.

After college, Pennebaker married, but within a few years his marriage started to feel like it was coming apart, which sent him into a spiral of depression. He started smoking. He drank more. He stopped eating. Then after a month he started writing, first about his marriage, then about his feelings, his parents, and his career, death, and so on.

"By the end of the week," he wrote, "I noticed my depression lifting. For the first time in years—perhaps ever—I had a sense of meaning and direction."[217] He realized he needed to stay with his wife, and things began to turn around.

In his research, Pennebaker wanted to explore these issues. So he and a graduate student designed an experiment where subjects would write about personal trauma from different perspectives. One group would vent about it. Another would recount the bare facts of the trauma. And a third group would delve into their emotions.

The students in the study did this for four days, fifteen minutes each day. They wrote about being sexually abused by relatives, about being told they caused their parents' divorce, about suicide attempts. One woman wrote that her own mother had told her to clean up her toys because her grandmother was coming over. She didn't, and her grandmother happened to slip on a toy, broke her hip, and died a week later.

The four days ended. Six months later, Pennebaker collected the records from the student health center. The results were shocking: In the months before the study, the students came to the health center at the same rate. But after the writing, students in the third group, "who wrote about their deepest thoughts and feelings," had a 50 percent drop in visits to the health center.[218]

A follow-up study showed the same thing: Students who wrote about "their deepest thoughts and feelings surrounding traumatic experiences" for twenty minutes a day for four days had blood drawn and showed a heightened immune function that lasted for six weeks. Those who wrote about superficial topics did not.[219]

It seemed that digging around in the roots of their stories had had profound effects on the students—effects that were biological and measurable. It suggested that when you pause to reckon with who you are—and what that means—a piece of bioloop grows stronger and then feeds that strength back into the whole.

The ability to see your own life story is a powerful thing,[220] but it's not always easy. In the times in my life when I've been depressed, it's felt like I didn't know what story I was part of, or that the one I was living was the wrong one, or that there was simply no audience for it at all. But in better times I could see myself as the protagonist in a grand adventure and realize how lucky I've been. I could see the threads, the meaning, and all the things below the surface.

While the notion that you can change your biology just by writing about your life a few times seems bizarre to most of us, it's precisely what's been found in the research on "affirmation theory," where subjects write short essays about their values (an act of affirming the self) and researchers look at the effects, which are surprisingly large. The affirmation essays are a window for self-reflection, a "psychological time-out: a moment to pull back and regain perspective on what really matters." This somehow improves the subjects' persistence, resilience, and health, sometimes for years.

In one experiment, students were given a writing assignment over their winter break. They wrote every other day for a total of ten assignments. In the first group, everyone wrote about their values. In the second, they wrote about "good things that were happening to them." In the third group, they wrote about another person—someone other than themselves. And in the last, no one wrote anything.

When the students returned from the break, the first group was the healthiest. They had fewer doctors' visits, fewer illness symptoms, and better health-related behaviors. The researchers found that students who used more words related to self-reflection, causation, achievement, and striving (words that are the backbone of storytelling) had a greater decrease in illness. This suggested those who were "attempting to understand and find causal meaning in their experience" acquired greater health benefits.[221]

Somehow, composing the story of yourself, tinkering with it, thinking about it, has a consolidating effect. The same way we look for causal cohesion in the world around us, we look for it in our life. And when we find it, or perhaps even when we just look for it, good things happen in our biology. When the human organism sees reasons to carry on, some ancient survival mechanisms kick in.

This is why so many people write memoirs, and why psychotherapy works (and indeed, it's why all 400 kinds of psychotherapies work equally well).[222] This is also probably why a new technique called Narrative Exposure Therapy (NET) has proven surprisingly effective for people suffering from PTSD in places like the war zones of northern Uganda.[223]

In NET, patients (many with extremely brutal backgrounds—like former child soldiers) are asked to tell their life story, focusing on the good and bad events in their lives and reliving these vividly. The idea behind it is that emotionally "hot" memories are too painful to be incorporated into a person's narrative, which makes their stories jagged and unformed.

They lay a rope across the floor, and for each good thing that happened to them, they place a flower on the rope. For each bad thing, they place a stone. By the end the fragmented memories of trauma are "transformed into a coherent narrative."[224]

The story of a Somali boy treated at a refugee camp in Uganda illustrates the point. At first he could think of only two stones and no flowers. One stone was for the day his parents were shot in front of him and he escaped through a back door, leaving a brother and a sister behind. The other stone was for the day he arrived in Nairobi to survive on the streets.

Eventually he was able to come up with a handful of flowers—playing soccer with his father before he was killed; meeting a group of Somalis in Kampala who took him in and helped him. After just four sessions, his PTSD had abated and he started talking about finding his siblings. Nine months later, he was well dressed and well fed. He'd grown taller, had put on weight, and was finishing his primary school. He'd even joined a soccer team; before the therapy, he'd refused to socialize with anyone.[225]

I'd never been through a war or a genocide or a disaster that would call for these kinds of interventions. But I did feel that I'd been doing something similar ever since I came home from Italy, trying to find the rope running through my life; trying to see how I got to the present, and where it would lead into the future. For years, I did this by following the stories of others, by tracing their paths. These took me some way down the road I wanted to be on. But in the end I had to veer off, to ask my own questions, to find my own way. That's why I went to Nigeria. That's why I'd come to China: to follow this story I'd started all the way through to its end.

12

THE WORM TURNS

Marian and I met early in the morning and taxied over to the other side of town. There we found a car heading to Lin'gao. Already, in the parking lot, I had the feeling of not exactly being in China. The two men with whom we shared the car had darker skin and looked more like they'd come from southern Thailand or Malaysia, not from China. We drove on a new freeway, through fields of palm trees and grasses. The new road was smooth and fast, and in about an hour we arrived in Lin'gao. It was a dusty town full of low, plain-looking buildings—a long way from the slick high rises and new money of Haikou.

As we rolled into town, I called Dennis, our guide and interpreter, then gave the phone to our driver, who spoke to Dennis in Lin'gaohua. The car stopped and we stepped out. He was easy to spot—a young, clean cut man, with glasses and an eager smile. He had gone to university on the other side of the island, then returned to Lin'gao to work as an English teacher. He was also trying to tutor himself in French.

"Okay," he said. "Where is our first destination? Would you like to go to the hospital to ask about this disease?"

"Yes," I said. "Of course."

The hospital was always the first stop. After all, that was where sick people ended up. And it had long been established that *koro* was a sickness, a disease, even though I felt uneasy whenever the term was used. But calling it a "delusion" wasn't right either. It felt more like something in between, for which there was no perfect word.

We crossed the Wenlan River and parked in the hospital's lot. It was a run-down place with broken tiles in the floor and dirty walls. Any resemblance to Guangzhou's shiny palaces of traditional and Western medicine was impossible to see.

The hospital's waiting area was a forest of IVs attached to people who turned their heads to stare at our party. Dennis made a few inquiries, and we climbed the stairs. In the hallway, we came to a doctor who sat at a desk. He did not give us his name and kept his face mask on while we spoke. Dennis showed him one of the studies I had on the Lin'gao epidemic and explained what we were looking for. I heard the word *suo yang*, but wasn't sure how or if this was translatable into Lin'gaohua. The doctor shook his head and said he hadn't heard anything about it. He told us we should go to the mental hospital in Haikou, since this was a mental problem.

Was that it? Was that all there was in Lin'gao, the epicenter of the 1984 epidemic? As we walked out of the hospital, I turned to Dennis.

"Is there any kind of traditional healer we could talk to?" I asked.

"You mean traditional Chinese medicine?"

"Yes, or if someone has problems with ghosts or something?"

"There is one in my village. Would you like to go talk to him?"

"Yes."

Outside in the bright southern sun, we found a taxi to take us to Dennis's village. As we were driving out of town, I asked if we could stop at one of the shops selling traditional medicinal herbs. We pulled over. The shop was dark inside. The counter was piled with bags of dried plants. Behind it stood a plump, middle-aged man. Along the wall were drawers full of herbs and other medicinal things.

I asked Dennis to ask the man if he had heard of *suo yang*. He did so, then turned back to me.

"He told me that with that kind of psychological problem it's not a real thing. And some other people told me they've never seen these ghosts, or this disease. It's just a tale."

"So do people in Lin'gao believe more in traditional Chinese medicine or Western medicine?" I asked.

"The younger people," he said, "they believe Western medicine is better than Chinese medicine. But the older people, they prefer the traditional medicine."

"Do you ever come here?" I asked.

"Me?"

"Yes."

"Sometimes."

"For what?"

"If I have some disease or any headache I will come to the hospital for urgent things. But in daily life, I would like to have some Chinese medicine for my best health. Chinese medicine can help with good health, and in daily life. But it cannot cure a disease."

"Do you know what this woman's problem is?" I asked, nodding toward the limping woman at the counter.

"Her leg had something wrong. It's very painful for her, but she doesn't know what it is. It's very awful. And he is making some medicine to cure it. In Lin'gao, or China, many local people, common people, use this way to protect themselves. You know Western medicine can do a little harm to the body.

Chinese medicine seems to have less harm. But Chinese medicine takes a long time to cure."

Back in the car. I told Dennis to ask the driver if he'd ever
heard of *suo yang*. The driver said no, then grew quiet.

We drove out of town and into the countryside, through
fields of rice and sugarcane and fruit trees. Dennis's village
was a small place surrounded by farmland. The air was still.
The houses were made of stone.

We walked up the main road to a compound. Dennis
entered and we saw an old man seated next to a wall with two
plastic buckets in front of him. It looked like a peasant's home,
except for the shiny chrome door on the cinder block house.
The man did not look up as Dennis talked to him. Then he
stood up slowly and motioned for us to follow him into the
house. Inside, we sat down.

"What do you want to know about traditional Chinese
medicine?" Dennis asked.

"Does he know about the *suo yang* and the foxy lady?"
(This was what Dennis called the fox spirit that was said to
roam the island.)

"And another?"

"Does he remembers 1984, when people had *suo yang*?"

"And another?"

"Do people today still have problems with ghosts?"

The old man and Dennis talked for a while, then he
turned to me.

"I'm sorry, he has never seen that," he said. "Maybe it's
a long time. When that happened, he was just a little child.
So he didn't know that. And later these things haven't ever
happened again."

"He doesn't know about the foxy lady?"

"No, he never knows this."

"And he's never treated somebody with *suo yang*?"

"In Hainan, or Lin'gao, these things were just a funny thing. Some people have heard about this, but some have not ever heard it. So even doctors like him have never seen this."

"So what does he do?"

"He can align the force of qi. If someone's leg is hurt he can cure it. If you fall down and your head hurts, he can find some medicine to cure it. Internal injuries, he can cure this. He is the only one."

"Does he use any local plants?"

"He uses plants. He uses the root of the plant. Or flowers to heal, to cure."

"Does he collect them?"

"Yes. He goes out to look for them on the earth, on the ground."

This was all frustrating and, I suspected, not true. The old man must have heard about *suo yang* at some point.

To outsiders, sometimes the door to a culture is simply closed, or there's no door at all—not even a window. Other times the only way in is through a language that it takes years to learn and even longer to understand. I took a different tack.

"So he can't help people who have problems with ghosts, or anything like that?"

Dennis brightened. "In this village, there are some people to do those things to frighten the ghosts. Some people do this for their career."

"Who?"

"In this village?"

"Yes. Can we talk to that person?"

"You want to speak to them?"

"Yes."

"Okay."

We went back out to the road, now with a couple of Dennis's friends in tow. The village was still eerily quiet, except for the wind in the trees. There was a group of old people sitting around in the midday sun, chatting in Lin'gaohua. Few of them spoke any Mandarin.

We followed Dennis to the end of the village where the ghost hunter lived. He had a good-size house near a new temple that was under construction. The man's wife, a small, smiling woman, greeted us. She talked loudly with Dennis for a few minutes.

"The man, he can't come back right now," Dennis said. "He has something to do. He is very far away. We can't go there."

"Can his wife tell us about what he does?" I asked.

Dennis paused, hesitated. "Actually, nobody here knows this. It's just a little mysterious."

"Maybe she can just tell me how many people he helps in like a month?"

"Many people!" Dennis said, without asking her. "Sometimes many people need them to do this. Sometimes maybe just no one."

I had the feeling there was more going on beneath the surface than I could see. Marian felt it too. Even for her, a professional translator who had lived in China for years, things felt strangely opaque. We had driven an hour, but gone so much farther.

"Just so I understand," I said, "if someone has a ghost in their house . . ."

"Yes," Dennis said. "Sometimes this man must go to people's houses, maybe to pre—let me see this word." He looked in his dictionary, flipped through the pages. "Sometimes, people . . ." He trailed off.

"How can we find someone to ask about this?" I pressed.
I had the feeling that, as in Alagbado, in Nigeria, I was close
to this other place and I couldn't just leave. There were no
Area Boys here—no threats—only the foxy lady, off somewhere roaming the countryside with her basket of members.

"He could come back in an hour . . . or tomorrow," Dennis said.

"Would it be possible to go to where this man is, to the
activity?"

"They do this tomorrow. Today they prepare for it. We
can see them. This activity would be done tomorrow morning."

"What happens tomorrow?"

"If someone dies, in one year, or two years, they do this
activity to show, to move the dead people's soul. Because in
Chinese culture, they think if you die your soul is wandering
around everywhere. So they want to do this activity to move
the soul."

A small crowd had gathered around us, curious as to what
two foreigners were doing so far from any city.

I turned to Dennis. "Do any of these people know about
the foxy lady?"

"Okay, let me ask them."

He turned and talked to some of the group. An old
woman laughed. He turned back to me.

"They have never heard about it."

"Let's wait for the man," I said.

"I don't know when he will come back. If I find out this
thing about the ghost I will send an e-mail to you."

I made a noncommittal sound and walked away. Dennis
left us. I wandered around, waiting. I couldn't leave until I
talked to the ghost hunter. Marian lay down on a concrete
platform and slept. The afternoon seemed to be moving in

slow motion. The crowd of old people lost interest in us and went back to their gossip. Then, sometime later, the ghost hunter just appeared.

He was a thin man with close cropped hair, graying around the edges. He had deep smile lines around his eyes. His voice was soft but firm, and he took an occasional drag on his cigarette.

Dennis reappeared and introduced us. We shook hands and he welcomed us into his house, which was dark. In the middle of the room was a coffee table, and high on the wall was a photo of Mao Zedong, who, in some rural villages, is equated with the healing god *Zhong Kui*: Mao the healer.[226]

We sat down around a coffee table in the middle of the room. The old man smiled. I had the feeling that he often sat around this table with people who needed something from him. It seemed like he was used to listening.

"Tell me your questions," Dennis said, ready to translate my questions and the old man's answers.

"I was wondering how often, or how many people, ask him for help with these ghost problems."

"Maybe three or so, in ten days or half a month. Sometimes it happens too much. So many people come to him."

"What does he do if people have a problem like this?"

"He will go to their homes to do this. Sometimes to the wide open fields. Just yesterday they went to prepare a big activity. And tomorrow they will begin to do it."

"What do they do? Light fireworks? Say a prayer?"

"Each time they do that, his work would be at the end. He has three incenses that he lights. And you can put the incense into something like this. Each person will use three incenses. And you can sit next to them and you can make a wish or anything. Each time people do this, we kill a chicken or get some pork or anything, and after we finish this, the owner of the house will give some money to him."

"Why kill the chicken?"

"In our minds, we believe the people who died have nothing to eat. So they put this out so the dead can eat. Then the leader will do the fireworks and we give him some money. And our activity has ended."

"And the ghost has gone from the house."

"Yes."

"Has he heard of the foxy lady ghost?"

"He says the foxy lady is just a tale. He has heard of it, but he has never seen it before."

"Does he ever have people ask him about the foxy lady ghost, people who are afraid of it?"

"No. No one. He hasn't heard this. Because the foxy lady happened in the fifties, sixties, and seventies, and at that time he was young and he didn't hear of it.

"So *suo yang* he's never heard of?"

"No, no."

"Does it ever happen that a ghost attacks a person?"

"In our tradition, if someone has diseases, a ghost must have touched him, and he would like to do an activity to let the ghost be away. But they don't know if the ghosts are a real thing or just a tale. The ghosts have never talked to people. So they don't know if it is a real thing or not."

"Did he say he doesn't know if they're real, or that they're not real?"

"He told me he doesn't know if the real ghosts exist or not. But in the people's hearts, they have the belief. It's just like this. And these days, people believe in Taoism. And the ghosts are Taoist ghosts. It's just one type of Taoism. So if people feel like they have a ghost troubling them, they want to do this to make the ghost get away. And it's just one belief. But the ghost is not real. Just like the God in America. I don't know if he really exists. But in people's hearts, they make a prayer like this?" He put his hands together and closed his eyes.

"Anything else?" he asked.

"No, I don't think so."

"So with this interview, are you happy?"

"Yes, very happy. Thank you."

Back in town, I asked Dennis if we could stop at a pharmacy. He nodded, and we pulled over and went into a small shop. The shelves were full of both Western and prepackaged Chinese medicines. The man at the counter had gray hair, but was not old. He and Dennis talked for a few minutes, before Dennis turned to me.

"He said he heard of *suo yang*, but he's never seen it. There was a place where it happened, and one man died, in a place near the shore. It happened a few years ago."

Outside, we said goodbye to Dennis, and to Lin'gao. He smiled and waved as we pulled away. After a few minutes, the driver turned to Marian and said something in Mandarin about *suo yang*. He told her his older brother had had it. He said it was not what we thought. She translated this for me.

"He said that some older people who don't believe in superstitions, they said that it was a worm."

"A worm?" I said. They spoke again.

"When you are sleeping," she explained, "the worm climbs in through your mouth and nose when you're breathing."

"Does he believe in the worm?"

"He can't say 'believe' or 'not believe.' It's real."

"Is he afraid of the worm?"

"Nobody has it any more. It's gone. But in the past, people were very, very afraid of it.

"And his brother had it?"

"Yes."

"And he recovered?"

"Yeah, he got better."

"What did he do to get better?"

"He was a small kid. He doesn't know, he said. He didn't ask his brother that. But he could call him now and ask him."

The driver dialed some numbers and talked to his brother for a while. Then he hung up and turned back to Marian.

"He said he had to do something that—I don't understand the word—but eventually something came out. A thing."

"The worm?"

"He's not sure either. But after he woke up, he basically didn't have anything."

"In Lin'gao?"

"Yes. In 1985, or maybe 1987. He remembered when we were all talking about it. And over a five-day period, there was another person who had it. And when one person had it, a lot of people would have it. They would do something with hot peppers."

We drove on. I looked out the window at the fields of palm trees. There was no mention of a worm in any of the literature I had read. Something had changed. Either a ghost had become a worm, or there had been even more stories than anyone had known. A worm was a physical cause, much different than a ghost. Yet ghosts were still there. Were they losing their power? Or were the stories changing to match the times?

As always, just when I thought I knew the direction this stream flowed, I found myself in water that was much deeper.

13

BEYOND BELIEF

All the way back to Haikou, I thought about worms and ghosts, and I wondered what these stories said about this landscape, about the world. They gave me the sense that we all swim in an ocean of stories, of currents—some visible, some hidden. They rise and fall like the tides. Sometimes they wash over us. Sometimes they pull us out to sea. Usually, we sail smoothly along, but we can always feel their pull.

That was what I'd felt in Italy, in Nigeria, at my brother's church, everywhere: the pull of stories around me, the way that they can be both powerful and contagious, and the way they flow between us. That was how *koro* had spread across Hainan all those years ago: People heard stories about it. They believed them. They feared them. They felt them.

The closer I got to these epidemics, the more I could see the resemblance they bore to another kind of illness I'd come across in my research, known as "mass psychogenic illnesses," in which a group of people are suddenly stricken with a mysterious illness, which they either saw or heard about.

Mass psychogenic illnesses are well known in the scientific literature. They spread through tight knit social groups, affect mostly females, and are common in Asia and Africa. In 2008, at a garment factory outside Jakarta, Indonesia, approximately fifty female workers went into a collective trance, weeping and jerking their bodies. In 2006, thirty women experienced a similar epidemic in a cigarette factory in Java. And again in 2008 in Kalimantan, on the Indonesian side of Borneo, thirty high school students also fell into a collective trance.[227]

These happen in our culture as well, and they may even be on the rise. In 2014, thirty students at a Minnesota high school became ill and were hospitalized with what they thought was carbon monoxide poisoning, but for which all tested negative.[228] The cause was psychogenic. In 2013 in Danvers, Massachusetts, two dozen teenagers at an agricultural school started developing strange hiccups and vocal tics that were eventually ruled to be a mass psychogenic illness.[229] In 2011, eighteen girls from a high school in LeRoy, New York, developed uncontrollable facial tics, muscle twitching, and garbled speech.[230] All physical causes were ruled out and the epidemic was declared to be a "psychogenic movement disorder" or "psychogenic parkinsonism."

These are not usually considered cultural syndromes, but they share key similarities with them: The symptoms are real, they are contagious, and they have some perceived cause at their root. It's usually poison or pollution in the West and spirits or spells in Africa and Asia. But in every case the process is the same: Victims learn the story, intuit the cause, and the looping begins. The mind starts to affect the body in tangible ways. It's like a compressed version of storytelling: Observed events, perceived causes, internalized effect.

But it is not just tics and nausea that can flow through us this way. For example, not long after the reunification of Germany in 1990, a national health survey was conducted and it was found that the two regions had starkly different rates of lower back pain, with a disparity as high as 16 percent.

Lower back pain is notoriously complicated. No one is sure what causes it. Risk factors include depression, nicotine dependence, obesity, alcohol abuse, and low social status. East and West Germany were not that different culturally, despite forty-five years of division, yet something was causing West Germans to have more back pain than East Germans.

A decade later that disparity was gone. The rates in East and West had converged. After unification, those in the former communist country rose steadily until 1996, when they began to track with the rates in West Germany. After that, they moved in unison.

Researchers were baffled, especially since, as they noted, "Between 1991 and 2003, the data show a slow increase in both general life satisfaction and job satisfaction in the East and a continually slow decrease in the West."[231] So the effects on people's lower backs should have been the opposite. Other possible factors included selective migration and increased unemployment in the East. But the authors of the paper (titled "Back Pain, a Communicable Disease?") ultimately suggested another factor: "after reunification, all [the] 'back myths' and misconceptions about back pain pervasive in Western societies were immediately disseminated in East Germany."[232]

The notion of lower back pain spreading from West Germany to East Germany culturally—passing from mind to mind—is hard for people in biomedical cultures to swallow. But that same kind of flow has been seen in other conditions, most notably in the Framingham Heart Study. What's even more interesting are the paths they take.

In 2007, researchers Nicholas Christakis and James Fowler looked at the health records of 12,067 people in the study and found a strange thing: Obesity did not—as expected—spread geographically. It spread socially: If you had a friend who became obese, your chance of following suit rose 57 percent. This was greater than the effect of a sibling (40 percent) or even a spouse (37 percent). The weight of a neighbor seemed to have no effect. Crucially, the flow was "directional" from people who were named as friends to those who named them and *not* the other way around.[233] So it wasn't just a matter of people who knew each other changing their diets and becoming obese at the same time. One person was *causing* the other to change. One person was *learning* from the other. Obesity, like *koro*, like psychogenic Parkinsonism, like back pain, could be contagious.

Christakis and Fowler went on to examine how smoking spread in a similar way: If a person quits smoking, there is a 67 percent chance his or her spouse would quit smoking—the effect of a friend quitting was 36 percent, while siblings were at 34 percent.[234] Another study of the data found that divorce flowed through the networks, too: If a friend or family member got divorced, your chance of getting divorced rose from 9 percent to 16 percent. If a friend of a friend got divorced, your chance of divorce rose to 12 percent.[235] After the third degree of separation (as with obesity and smoking), there was no effect. Other research has shown that happiness,[236] loneliness,[237] and depression[238] flow this way as well. Christakis and Fowler call this the "peer effect," while others call it the "interpersonal health effect." The theorist Gustave LeBon would have simply called it "social contagion," but in other fields, it's been described as "observational learning," or "social learning."[239]

Placebo expert Fabrizio Benedetti has found that watching someone experience pain (or feel pain relief) has a much larger placebo/nocebo effect than merely being told about it. Watching someone in pain causes "negative emotional contagion," he writes, which kickstarts the mechanisms that cause pain in the observer as well.[240] Stories we hear are never as powerful as the ones we see.[241] That is the secret of the peer effect, of social contagion, and of mass psychogenic illness. That's why it's so hard to resist the pull of the cultures we are in.

We watch the people in our lives. We learn the way things go, the scripts, the schemas, the patterns: How to get something at the store. How to talk to someone you love. How to get through your day. How to get through your life. As Dan McAdams says, "people pick and choose and plagiarize selectively from the many stories and images they find in culture to formulate a narrative identity."

Except the stories are not *in* the culture. They *are* the culture.[242]

When I went to Italy I realized that there were so many ways to be, to act, to think, to speak, and to live in this world. When I came home, I had the arbitrary task of choosing the scripts worth keeping, and those worth discarding. How is a nineteen-year-old supposed to decide that? How do you know the best way to live, which path to take? For me, it felt like the old roads had closed, while new ones were endless. And that endlessness was terrifying.

The only way I could see forward was as a writer. I didn't know why, but it seemed like that was the kind of life that would allow me to figure these things out, to explore the world, to understand, to make sense. So when Paul Gruchow came to our class, I saw what I needed to see: living proof (despite his warnings) that such an existence was possible; that such a story could be written.

For years it was brutal, heartbreaking, just as Gruchow had warned. It never went like I'd planned. But over time I began to meet more writers, and I started to realize that there was no secret, no template, no master plan, no guarantee. Everyone who did this had to start from the beginning. There were no rules other than hard work and delusional self-belief, which I had. Every writer's story was a mongrel pastiche. Everyone had to take something old and make it new. This didn't make it easier, but by the time I realized it, I had already traveled a long way down my own road.

Yet even knowing all this, I was surprised when I saw the headline: AUTHOR PAUL GRUCHOW, WHO CHRONI-CLED THE PRAIRIE, DIES AT 56.[243] There were few details. He'd been deeply depressed and had taken his life with a drug overdose. Not long before he died, an old friend wrote to ask if he could write a story about him. Gruchow responded, "Last year I earned $62.85 in royalties and gave one public talk, in Duluth, that drew a dozen listeners . . . Two or three times the phone rings. Usually I don't answer it. There isn't a story."[244]

There was a story, just not one he wanted to tell. It almost certainly wasn't the one he'd imagined when he first dreamed of becoming a writer. I still wonder if it was the story he'd been trying to tell me years earlier, when I sat across from him at his home, full of hope.

The stories we believe, the scripts we follow, the syndromes we suffer are all made up of the pieces we find floating around us. We bind them together to help us float down the river of stories, though we never quite know how far we will go, if our knots will hold, or where we will wash ashore.

14

TO THE SEA

The bus rolled out of Haikou toward the southern town of Sanya, where there were rumors of recent *koro* epidemics. Out the window, I could see how much of the countryside had been flattened by the hurricane the week before. As we climbed into the foothills, the TV at the front of the bus played *mandopop* videos, followed by a dubbed Chinese version of *Avatar*, for which language wasn't necessary.

The bus ascended into the mountains, which loomed jagged and green in the darkening sky. We wound along a small road for nearly five hours until we came to the town of Wuzhishan, where I met a friend of Marian's named Frank Ji, who ran a bike touring company there.

Frank picked me up on his motorcycle and took me to a couple hotels, none of which would let me check in, citing defunct Cold War–era restrictions on foreigner visitors. So Frank let me sleep on his couch in the cavernous room where he kept the high-end bikes he rented to the Chinese tourists who flocked to the island in winter months. Once that same room had been Wuzhishan's cultural museum, and parts of the native village diorama still stood in the back corner.

The next morning, Frank and I biked up into the Five Finger Mountains. It was green and lush and quiet. There were hardly any cars. Around us, the forest changed as we climbed, growing denser. Finally we stopped in an actual native village called Shuiman.[245] The buildings were painted with angular pictograms that looked like they belonged in Indonesia. According to Edward Schafer in *Shore of Pearls*, the area around Shuiman was once "the inaccessible and ultimate stronghold of the native people,"[246] in their rebellion against the Chinese.

Frank was from the northern city of Handan—near Beijing—a steel-manufacturing area. He grew up breathing air that was thick with smog and watching rivers run black from industry. When he got a chance to study at the University in Wuzhishan, he was thrilled.

"When I saw all the green," he told me, "I never wanted to leave."

After a few months, however, he realized he wasn't going to learn much English at school, so he dropped out and spent several years watching American movies on video. He learned so much, and now speaks so well, that he's become one of the most sought after interpreters in the province.

Back at his place that evening, I told him about *suo yang*, which he hadn't heard of. He immediately got online and started researching it.

"It happened in village after village for one year." He read from a Chinese language report on the 1984–85 epidemic, "In total it happened in sixteen counties. And more than three thousand people. The first records of it happening is in 1861. And also in 1908, they have records about it happening in Taiwan. It says this kind of disease can attack a group of people together, or some individuals. And also, it's not only China. It's Thailand, Singapore, Malaysia, Indonesia, and India, and some records in Russia in 1885 and 1886."

He read on.

"The patient may be having an illusion, seeing weird things, hearing weird sounds. And he sees some spirit, and is smelling a spirit. All these patients, they believe what is happening is real, and that they are about to die. And in that situation, they lose their mind. They don't care about the people are around them. They will take off their clothes and hold on to their penis. So it's mainly a mental disease, but it causes them to start shaking and sweat and cannot see things, and also get headaches, and the only physical thing is because they hold their penis so hard to hurt it. And it's mainly because of the culture, the background culture. Because Chinese people in the old culture—they think semen comes from blood. One drop of semen is ten drops of blood. So they're thinking, if you have masturbated, you cost a lot of energy and blood. And your kidney will get low function. And so it's popular all around the street, a lot of the medicine to try to help people warm up their kidney."

He turned to me. "I guess they did too much hand work," he said, and laughed. Then he read on. "Also Chinese people believe that the animal's penis will help them to recover. So they eat animal penis and they drink some of this wine. They put the penis in the wine and drink the wine."

"In Singapore, one guy told me they use tiger penis."

"Yes, it's more powerful."

"Do they say that here, or do you just know that?"

"I just know it. It's kind of cultural. It also says in Indonesia and Malaysia, people believe if a woman dies during childbirth, or after they give birth to a child, their spirit will turn to evil ghosts. And they will hurt, especially the men."

"Right, and they come back as a vampire."

"And these vampires appear and can take away the penis and balls. They cut it off. And most of these things were caused by rumors. Because first it's a rumor, like *koro*, and people believe it, and maybe because of too much handwork, they are worried about themselves."

Frank read some statistics about the Hainan epidemic, including an elaborate village by village breakdown. After a while, though, he got bored, and found another article about a town on the island called Ledong, where a strange crime was being prosecuted: a woman's three sons were in jail after she had been burned alive. It was believed that the mother was possessed and that she would bring ruin to the family, so a local "sorcerer" tried to purge her with alcohol. The woman was "hit in the head, face, abdomen, etc. with palms, fists, sticks," and finally burned to death. The paper noted that though "the daughter of the deceased, three grandchildren, and a dozen relatives were at the scene, they did not stop this violence." Some of them even "shouted applause."

The paper editorialized: "These people's superstition, ignorance is shocking. How to strengthen rural scientific knowledge and legal advocacy?"[247]

Frank couldn't believe this event had taken place today in Hainan, with so many people there looking on. But for me, it wasn't so mysterious. By now the influence of others—the power of their words, the contagion of their stories, the infectiousness of their beliefs—had started to feel like a force of nature.

"Most people in Hainan," I told him, "believed *suo yang* was caused by the fox spirit."

Frank nodded. "That is a very common story in China: The fox gets to be one thousand years old, then turns into a beautiful woman, and no man can resist her. But everyone knows this is just a story, don't they?"

"Not everyone," I said.

• • •

The next morning, Frank had some business to attend to, so he made a few calls and found a young woman who studied English at the university who could help me translate. Her English name was Lacey. She was very eager and interested in *suo yang*, which, also being from the north, was new to her.

We met on the main road, not far from the steps that led up to the university. We caught a minibus out to the edge of Wuzhishan and got off across the street from the mental hospital. We walked into the empty lobby and heard footsteps. Across the room was a doctor walking through.

Lacey stopped him and gave a brief synopsis of what we were looking for. Then she turned to me.

"He said he doesn't see any patients here who have *suo yang*. But there were stories of it two or three years ago."

"Where?"

"Ledong."

"Is it far from here?"

"Maybe one hour by car. But he said he can ask someone who knows. He heard it from the president of the hospital!" She sounded excited. "He said he knows about these things. It's unbelievable. I've never heard about this before!"

The man motioned for us to follow him, and we went outside, to where the president stood talking to some other people at the entrance to the hospital. His name was Dr. Yang and he had a black leather jacket and slicked back hair. Again Lacey stepped up, talked to the president, then turned back to me.

"He says in five years he hasn't had any patients like that. But last year in Sanya, at the hospital like this, they did have patients. He said there are a few people there who know about this. He said maybe if we go to Sanya we can discover something about it. He thinks there were five or six people who had this *suo yang*."

Dr. Yang gave us directions and a name, and we quickly made arrangements to go to Sanya—there was a bus leaving in an hour. Lacey hurried back to her dormitory to grab some things, then met me at the bus stand.

The road was steep as it dropped from the mountains to the sea. Up front, the TV blared the same *mandopop* videos I'd seen before; by the time we arrived in Sanya, I was ready to never see them again. We got off in town. Lacey asked around and we started walking toward the hospital. The sidewalks were dense with large Russian tourists, who came for the sunshine and beaches that rivaled those anywhere in Thailand. Construction projects were underway everywhere. Sanya, too, was booming.

Soon we came to a sign that read SAN YA PREVENTION AND CURE OF CHRONIC DISEASE HOSPITAL. I wasn't sure it was the right place, but we went in and just down the main hall, we found the "Psychiatric Rehab Ilitation Clinic" (which doubled as the "skin sex disease room").

The room had one desk and no computers. Behind the desk sat a man named Dr. Zhen, who leaned back in his chair and motioned us to come in. Lacey explained our mission and he listened carefully, nodding. He said hadn't personally seen the patients Dr. Yang mentioned, but he knew it was the year before last.

"Did they come to this hospital?" I asked and Lacey translated.

"They would never come here," he said. "They never come to the doctor, They just use ginger or chili powder. Or they set fireworks all night to keep the spirits away. The government sent the doctors there."

"Does it happen in other parts of Hainan?" I asked.

"There are a lot of places on Hainan that have this, like Ledong and Sanya.

"Today or in the past?"

"Since 1985, every year we have some *suo yang* patients. But this year, not as much."

"Is it still something that spreads between people?"

"Mostly it happens to young people."

"Do they think it's the fox ghost, or what do they think is the cause?"

"Yes, or something like that."

"So it's still around in the small villages?"

"Yes."

"Because some people say *suo yang* is disappearing."

"I'm afraid not! It happens very frequently in some places more than others, like Ledong, Sanya, Danzhou."

"Do you remember the 1985 epidemic?" I asked.

"Yes!" he said. "That was when I first came to Sanya, in 1985. The whole village would be afraid and they would stay awake the whole night lighting fireworks."

"And what do you know about the most recent epidemic?"

"If you want to get more detailed information you can come back tomorrow. Or you can go to the Provincial Hospital in Haikou. They have a lot of information there. They are the ones who came to do the research."

We chatted for a little longer, but it seemed like we'd exhausted his knowledge of the most recent events so we thanked him and went back outside. I had to get back to Haikou. On the street, Lacey put me on a motorcycle to the high speed train.

"Thank you so much," she said before we parted. "This is very interesting! Today I learned so much about my country!"

I would hear from her again the next year by e-mail, when her friend from Ledong said there had been another epidemic: A woman playing cards had felt that her breasts were disappearing, and a panic, once again, spread through the town. I wondered if *suo yang* had actually declined or just disappeared from hospitals. In any case, it seemed like the old stories were still alive. Maybe there were still ghosts. Maybe genitals were still at risk. Maybe the world was not, and never would be, as flat as we wanted to believe.

The train traveled smoothly through the night. It was fast and clean and felt far removed from the fishing villages and roadless towns of Hainan's past. But I suspected the distance wasn't as great as it seemed. Some of those old streams still flowed down from the mountains out to the sea.

The next morning in Haikou, I went over to the provincial mental hospital with Marian's assistant, Sansa. It was a huge building on the edge of town. At the front desk, she asked where we would go to find out about *suo yang*, and we were sent to the psychiatry department upstairs. When we got there, Sansa explained what we were looking for and they sent us to the "Department of Psychosomatic Medicine," which, as far I could tell, had only one office.

Inside, we waited for a few minutes until the doctor (and department head) arrived. He was a slightly disheveled man in a white coat named Dr. Wu Chuandong. He was very keen to hear about my trip, since he had been researching *suo yang* for many years and had been the lead investigator in the most recent epidemic.

The first people who had *koro*, he said, were the people from Malaysia, who brought it to Hainan. For the last one hundred years, an epidemic had occurred every ten years after some big event, like a war. People would panic about their security and the body made certain changes.

"Do you remember the panic of 1984 and 1985?" I asked. Sansa translated.

"Yes. I went to that place to do the research, to interview people, for two years—up to 1987."

"And what did they feel was the cause? Did they feel like it was ghosts or the yang problem?"

"There was the story of the fox spirit," he said. "The fox wants to get more yang and heat from the virgins, male and female. And when he gets a certain amount of yang he can become a spirit and he can make the journey to the west, like an angel in heaven. So he can become a god and he can do whatever he wants. He can reach his goals."

"So in the villages people believed that was true?

"Yes. They believed that. And if they come from this cultural background, they have a high risk of catching *koro*."

"Do you remember anything about the people you interviewed? About the stories they told?"

"The people couldn't tell before it happened. You couldn't predict such a thing. It just happened. Some people find it happened when they bathed in the ocean, or when they took a shower, or when they needed to pee. They just knew that it became smaller and dragged them into this story. Then they got more panicked and more nervous about this. Then the whole village gets panicked and they would do something to avoid this, like hanging a red lantern on the gate. And also, sometimes very furious people, very angry people, they said virgin boys or girls can't go out together."

"And today do they still believe that happened, that the fox spirit was real?"

"The people in rural areas, in the villages where it happened, they prefer to believe in that legend, in that superstition."

"How has the situation changed since 1985?"

"We didn't hear of any cases until 2011, when eight or ten people in Sanya had such problems. And we went to interview them."

"What did those people think?" I asked.

"It was also a kind of rumor, like the fox story. Same style but not the same story. People said a spirit in the ocean took a boat to Sanya Bay and stayed there and it wants to be young and beautiful. It happened that a boy went out to play. The next morning, he woke up to pee and he found his penis had become smaller, and also he felt bad. His parents tried to pull it out, and they used a drum and cymbals, and they made noise to get the spirit to go away. And they used pepper on his penis to make the ghost go away.

"I see."

"And in the Sanya case, they are from Danzhou. People who are usually caught into this situation are speaking the Danzhou dialect. It may be something connected with Danzhou culture."

"Do you have any idea what has changed? Why is it not happening as much now?"

"It's because there is no rumor of the fox ghost or anything like that. There's no source of rumor and no atmosphere for rumor or anything like that, and so no cases."

"So if the rumor came, it would happen again? Or has the culture changed so people don't believe rumors like that anymore?"

"The culture is still the same. People still have the possibility to believe these rumors. I don't know if you can change people's minds. It takes a longer time to change the culture and their minds. So they just forbid people from spreading the rumors."

"And the belief is still strong in Danzhou?"

"It's a cultural thing, and Danzhou people mostly believe that some evil things will come to a village to get the young virgin boys, so he can be much more spirit. Most people who had this in 1984 and 1985 were from Danzhou."

"And you think the decline is not because of cultural change, but because of the lack of rumors."

"The culture changes when people change their minds. But it is difficult to change that. The government, and the doctors, go to the rural places and educate people, to explain from medical theory that your penis cannot shrink into your body. But the people still believe. I think we need more research on the people who get *koro*, on what kind of people they are. I am very curious why, in such modern times, people believe these stories."

We thanked Dr. Wu and left. And as we walked back across town, the wind blew around us. I thought about his last question, which had once been mine too. But I realized that I didn't wonder why anymore. Because I knew that people believed these stories in such modern times for the same reason we have always believed any stories. They hold our worlds together. They hold our selves together. They're the raft on which we steer our lives down the river. If it falls apart, if we abandon it, if it's destroyed on the rocks, all we can do is swim.

ACKNOWLEDGMENTS

How can you thank everyone who has ever helped you, from the time you were eighteen years old until you were forty-four? That's what this feels like, since this book—short as it is—was written over such a long time with the help of so many people. I'm terrified of leaving anyone out, and if I do I hope you will forgive me. So here goes:

In Bologna, Filippo Nonni and my classmates at San Luigi pulled me through a tough year and made sure my Italian was as colorful as possible. The Westricks, whose generosity changed my life, will always be family. I'm still sorry about the dog I brought home. (And the passport.)

In college, before I had any business writing anything, I received encouragement from Professors Jim Heynen, Eric Nelson, and others. In Tanzania, I would not have survived without Shoonie Hartwig, Dora Kripapuri, Royce and Sandy Truex, Dee and Pete Cresswell, Elisa Meier, Pam Boyd, Juliette Lyimo, and my students and neighbors.

In Portland, I owe a deep debt to my coworkers at Powell's City of Books (including the alumni of "Team Fun"), as well as to Bill Donahue, who first showed me what it meant to be a writer (and a friend), and to Dave Dranchak for late-night discussions about extraterrestrial life. In Madison, Jason Daley and Mukoma wa Ngugi kept me sane, as did Rae Meadows, Alex Darrow, Stephanie Fiorelli, and Adam Koehler (all of whom later let me freeload in New York). Also in Wisconsin,

Michael Perry showed me what it meant to be not only a great writer, but also a great person.

In Nigeria, none of this would have been possible without the ubiquitous Toni Kan, the lovely Wendy Onwordi, and the unflappable Akeem. Thanks to Helon Habila for sending me in the right direction, as well as to Jossy Idam, Starrys Obazi, Mike Jimoh, and Wasiu Karimu, wherever he is . . . hopefully intact.

In Minneapolis, Jason Albert, Doug Mack, Maggie Ryan Sandford, Dennis Cass, Lars Ostrom, Sara Aase, Ashley Shelby, and Jason Good gave me invaluable feedback. Michael Fuerstein tutored me philosophically, while Daniel Slager and Kelly Barnhill offered sage publishing advice. And of course thanks to the Minnesota State Arts Board, who want me to say: "Frank Bures is a fiscal year 2014 recipient of an Artist Initiative grant from the Minnesota State Arts Board. This activity is made possible by the voters of Minnesota through a grant from the Minnesota State Arts Board, thanks to legislative appropriation by the Minnesota State Legislature; and by a grant from the National Endowment for the Arts." Also, key parts of this book were written at the Anderson Center in Red Wing, Minnesota.

On the road: In Singapore, thanks to Dean Visser and Jacques van Wersch for logistical and linguistic aid. In China, thanks to Arthur Kleinman and Pete Hessler for helping me make connections, and to Marian Rosenberg, without whom navigating Hainan would have been a Kafkaesque nightmare. Huge thanks to the intrepid Sansa Wang in Haikou, to Frank Ji in Wuzhishan, to my translators Lacey, Dennis, and Shirley, as well as the lovely staff of the Lazy Gaga in Guangzhou.

Elsewhere, thanks to Bill Wasik for seeing the potential

in a story when no one else did, and to Tom Bissell for opening that door. Thanks to Eileen Cope for shepherding this project all the way through, to David Farley for hospitality and camaraderie, to Umberto Squarcia and Lissette Merlano for letting me crash in your increasingly crowded home. Thanks to Teju Cole for keeping this story alive and to Ellie Robbins for seeing bigger things in it. Thanks of course to fellow travelers Jim Benning, Mike Yessis, Rolf Potts, Eva Holland, Chris Vourlias, and all the World Hum gang. And thanks as well to the scientists who offered their time and ideas for this project: Arthur Kleinman, Daniel Moerman, Ted Kaptchuk, Peter Guarnaccia, Roberto Lewis-Fernandez, Devon Hinton, Heiner Raspe, Jamie Pennebaker, Peter Logan, Andrew Gordan, Dan McAdams, Chris Dowrick, Jan Brunvand, Shelley Adler, Julian Leff, Graham Thurgood, and Wolfgang Jilek. You are doing the real work from which the rest of us benefit. I hope I have done your ideas and research justice.

A huge thanks to Mark Krotov for his deft and insightful editing, and to all the lovely people at Melville House who helped bring this book into the world. Thanks to Marian Rosenberg, Ted Barnhill, and my mother for flawless proofreading and for delivering me (mostly, I hope) from typos. And thanks to Shiva Naipaul for showing what is possible.

Of course, thanks to my parents, Frank and Ruth Bures, for shipping me overseas to a country where I could legally drink, for their constant support in so many forms, and for being there even when I didn't deserve it, which was most of the time. Thanks to my brothers Bob and Joe, for putting up with my crap, and to their wives, Anna and Karen, for putting up with my brothers. Thanks to my mother-in-law, Judy Flaten, for covering for me while I was gone. Thanks to my in-laws John Jordan and Marianne Zerbe, for letting me abuse their generosity and for believing in this story early on, despite much evidence to the contrary.

To my two daughters, who brighten everything with their humor and enthusiasm, thanks for enduring my absences, not to mention all the talk about penis stealing taking the "embarrassing Dad" thing to another new level.

But most of all thanks to my brilliant and beautiful wife, Bridgit, who has endured years of semicoherent rambling about missing genitals, obscure medical trivia, half-baked theories, and who manages to pretend to still be interested after all these years. She has always been, and remains, the center of my world. I couldn't do any of this without her.

NOTES

Chapter 1: The Case of the Missing Manhood

1. Kunle Adeyemi, "Court Remands Man Over False Alarm on Genital Organ Disappearance," *The Punch*, October 21, 2005, p. 5.

2. Mannir Dan-Ali, "Missing penis sparks mob lynching," *BBC News*, April 12, 2001.

3. "Benin alert over 'penis theft' panic," *BBC News*, November 27, 2001.

4. The friend of a friend was Helon Habila, whom I interviewed for *Poets & Writers Magazine*. He was one of the first people I remember talking to who saw his life as a story. As he told me, "You see, literature is ordered. You have your beginning. You have your middle. You have your ending. You have your story. You have your plot. Everything follows. Everything falls into place . . . Then we live a happy life. We have a good moment at the end." (Frank Bures, "Everything Follows: An Interview with Helon Habila," *Poets & Writers Magazine*, January/February 2003).

5. Basher, T. A. "The Influence of Culture on Psychiatric Manifestations," *Transcultural Psychiatry*, 1963, No. 15, pp. 51–51. Cited in Pow Meng Yap, "Koro—A Culture-bound Depersonalization Syndrome," *British Journal of Psychiatry*, 1965 (111), p. 48.

6. Sunday Ilechukwu, "*Koro*-like Syndromes in Nigeria," *Transcultural Psychiatric Research Review*, 1988; 25:310–4. Incidentally, Ilechukwu relocated to Michigan, where penises are not in danger from magic.

7. Sunday Ilechukwu, "Magical Penis Loss in Nigeria: Report of a Recent Epidemic of a *Koro*-like Syndrome," *Transcultural Psychi-*

atric Research Review, 1992, 29, pp. 91–108. See also: Ifabumuyi OI, Rwegellera GGC. *"Koro* in a Nigerian male patient." *African Journal of Psychiatry* 1979; 5, pp. 103–105.

8. Vivian Afi Dzokoto and Glenn Adams, "Understanding Genital Shrinking Epidemics in West Africa: *Koro,* Juju, or Mass Psychogenic Illness?" *Culture, Medicine and Psychiatry,* 29: pp. 53–78, 2005.

Chapter 2: Following Threads

9. In 1989, Winona was still an old, blue-collar river town where the wild side had never quite died. The red light district operated openly until 1942, when it was shut down by the State Bureau of Criminal Apprehension. But even after that, the town's festive culture endured and made it very different from Italy. (Frank Bures, "Brothels Once Thrived in Winona," *Winona Daily News* (Heritage Edition), September 21, 1997.)

10. See Gruchow's *Necessity of Empty Places,* and *Journal of a Prairie Year,* both published by Milkweek Editions.

11. For musing of this sort, see "Test Day: Frank Bures administers an English exam to his students in Tanzania, where life is hard and giving up isn't an option," *World Hum,* 2003: "On Tanzanian Time: In a land where they have a name for people who are always in a hurry—Mzungu!—Frank Bures meditates on the art of slowing down, *World Hum,* 2003; One Tough Bastard at the Metropole," *Brevity,* Issue 9.

12. After we left, I salvaged this assignment for the *Christian Science Monitor*: "Muslim Unrest Flares in Thailand: Two Policemen Were Killed Monday After Bangkok Declared Martial Law in the South, the Scene of Renewed Separatist Violence" (*Christian Science Monitor,* January 7, 2004: csmonitor.com /2004/0107/p06s01-wosc.html).

13. The school provided us with a bedroom, but it was packed with photos of the school's founder and his mother. We did have a small

kitchen. The sink drained into the shower so you had to pick rice out of your toes. Sometimes we would come home and find the entire staff milling around in our room. Worst of all, though, was the thin, partial wall between our bed and the headmaster's desk. It was awkward when he worked late.

14. A few years later, on *Granta*'s twenty-fifth anniversary in 2007, that same editor told *The Guardian*: "The worst thing is to commission a piece . . . and for it to come in after the writer has spent months on it, for it to be a long way short of the full shilling, so it goes back to the writer, and comes in again, and it's still not right, so it goes back for more work, and finally I have to say to the writer, 'I'm really sorry, this doesn't work.' It's absolutely defensible, but it's a soul-destroying thing for the writer." I knew who he was referring to.

15. Topics included a piccolo player harassing local shop owners, an interview with Tom Wopat (who went to the local university before starring in *The Dukes of Hazzard*), and profiling the local celebrity runner Suzy Favor Hamilton before she was interesting.

Chapter 3: Culture Bound

16. See also S. Mohammad Hatta, "A Malay Cross Cultural Worldview and Forensic Review of Amok," *Australian and New Zealand Journal of Psychiatry*, 1996; 30: pp. 505–10; also in Ronald C. Simons and Charles C. Hughes, *The Culture-Bound Syndromes: Folk Illnesses of Psychiatric and Anthropological Interest* (Dordrecht, The Netherlands: D. Reidel Publishing Company, 1985), pp. 197–269.

17. Lawrence Osborne, "Regional Disturbances," *New York Times Magazine*, May 6, 2001, p. 98. See also Robert Winzeler, *Latah in Southeast Asia: The History and Ethnography of a Culture-Bound Syndrome* (Cambridge: Cambridge University Press, 1995).

18. Stefan G. Hofmann and Devon E. Hinton, "Cross-Cultural Aspects of Anxiety Disorders," *Current Psychiatry Reports*, 2014, 16, p. 450.

19. Noriyuki Nakamoto et al., "Hikikomori: Is It a Culture-reactive

or Culture-bound Syndrome? Nidotherapy and a Clinical Vignette from Oman," *International Journal of Psychiatry in Medicine*, vol. 35(2), pp. 191–98, 2005; also in Maggie Jones, "Shutting Themselves In," *New York Times Magazine*, January 15, 2006, pp. 46–51.

20. Takahiro Takino, "Masked Social Withdrawal Liked to Japanese Culture," City News Department, *Mainichi Shimbun*, May 12, 2010.

21. Devon E. Hinton, Vuth Pich, Luana Marques, et al., "Khyâl Attacks: A Key Idiom of Distress Among Traumatized Cambodia Refugees," *Culture, Medicine and Psychiatry*, 2010, 34: pp. 244–78.

22. A. Sumathipala, S. H. Siribaddana, and Dinesh Bhugra, "Culture-bound Syndromes: The Story of Dhat Syndrome," *British Journal of Psychiatry*, 2004, 184: pp. 200–209. See also *Diagnostic and Statistical Manual of Mental Disorders*, 5th Edition. (Washington, D.C.: APA, 2013) p. 833.

23. D. Dutta, H. R. Phookan, and P. D. Das, "The *Koro* Epidemic in Lower Assam," *Indian Journal of Psychiatry*, 1982, 24(4), pp. 370–74.

24. A. N. Chowdhury, P. Pal, A. Chatterjee, M. Roy, and B. B. Das Chowdhury, "Analysis of North Bengal Koro Epidemic with Three Years Follow Up," *Indian Journal of Psychiatry*, January 1988; 30(1), pp. 69–72.

25. Akhilesh Jain, Kamal Kumar Verma, et al., "'Gilhari (Lizard) Syndrome': A New Culture Bound Syndrome," *Psychiatry: Open Access*, 2014, 17: 117. (Also previously published as K. K. Verma, M. M. Bhojak, and A. K. Singhal, "'Gilhari (Lizard) Syndrome'— is it a new culture bound syndrome?—A case report," *Indian Journal of Psychiatry*, 2001; 43(1): pp. 70–72.

26. Beng-Yeong Ng, "Wei Han Zheng (Frigophobia): A Culture-related Psychiatric Syndrome," *Australian and New Zealand Journal of Psychiatry* 1998; 32, p. 582.

27. Ted Kaptchuk, *Chinese Medicine: The Web That Has No Weaver* (London: Rider Books, 2000), pp. 437–52.

28. Moira Smith, "The Flying Phallus and Laughing Inquisitor: Penis

Theft in the Malleus Maleficarum," *Journal of Folklore*, 2002, vol. 39, no. 1, pp. 85–117; Kathleen Biddick, "Becoming Ethnographic: Reading Inquisitorial Authority in the Hammer of Witches," *Essays in Medieval Studies: Figures of Speech: The Body in Medieval Art, History, and Literature*, 1994, vol. 11, p. 30.

29. J. Guy Edwards, "The *Koro* Pattern of Depersonalization in an American Schizophrenic Patient," in *The Culture Bound Syndromes*, p. 167.

30. Wolfgang Jilek, "Epidemics of 'Genital Shrinking' (*Koro*): Historical Review and Report of a Recent Outbreak," *Curare*, 1986, vol. 9, p. 271.

31. Beng Yeong Ng and Ee Heok Kua, "*Koro* in Ancient Chinese History," *History of Psychiatry*, 1996(7), p. 565.

32. Ibid., p. 566.

33. Ibid.

34. Chris Buckle et al., "A Conceptual History of *Koro*," *Transcultural Psychiatry*, March 2007, 44, p. 30.

35. Ibid.

36. Arabinda N. Chowdhury, "Hundred Years of *Koro*: The History of a Culture-bound Syndrome," *International Journal of Social Psychiatry*, 1998(44), p. 181.

37. Wen-Shing Tseng, Mo Kan-Ming, et al., "A Sociocultural Study of *Koro* Epidemics in Guangdong, China," *The American Journal of Psychiatry*, December 1988; 145; 12, p. 1538; also in Jilek, 1986, p. 273.

38. Edward Rhodes Stitt, Richard Pearson Strong, Stitt's Diagnosis, Prevention and Treatment of Tropical Diseases, Volume 2, (Philadelphia: The Blakiston Company, 1942) p. 1145.

39. Laurence J. Kirmayer, "Cultural Psychiatry in Historical Perspective," Textbook of Cultural Psychiatry (Cambridge: Cambridge University Press, 2007), p. 8.

40. Helen F. K. Chiu, "Professor Pow-Meng Yap: A Giant in Psychiatry from Hong Kong," *Asia-Pacific Psychiatry*, 2012(4), pp. 84–86.

41. Pow Meng Yap, "Mental Diseases Peculiar to Certain Cultures: A Survey of Comparative Psychiatry," *The Journal of Mental Science*, April 1951, vol. XCVII, no. 407, p. 313.

42. Ibid., p. 327.

43. Ibid., pp. 314–15.

44. Pow Meng Yap, "*Koro*—A Culture-bound Depersonalization Syndrome," *British Journal of Psychiatry*, 1965(111), p. 48.

45. Arthur Kleinman and Robert Hahn, "Belief as Pathogen, Belief as Medicine: 'Voodoo Death' and the 'Placebo Phenomenon' in Anthropological Perspective," *Medical Anthropology Quarterly*, 1983; 14(4), pp. 3, 16–19.

46. Arthur Kleinman, *The Illness Narratives* (New York: Basic Books, 1988).

Chapter 4: Modern Minds

47. Cited in Will Durant's *The Story of Philosophy: The Lives and Opinions of the Great Philosophers* (New York: Simon & Schuster, 1933), p. 284.

48. When Yap arrived, Hong Kong was growing fast, modernizing faster, and well on its way to becoming one of the world's great cities, mixing parts of the world's cultures to become something all its own. During the Japanese Occupation in WWII, the population dropped from 1.6 million to 600,000. By 1948, just three years after the British reoccupied the colony, it was almost 2 million, with refugees from China's civil war pouring across the border. In 1966, the population hit 4 million. As of this writing in 2016, there are 7 million people living in its borders. (From the *Encyclopedia Britannica* [Chicago: Encyclopedia Britannica, 1968], vol. 11, p. 660, and the *CIA World Factbook*.)

49. Gruesome as it sounds, this was state of the art and a great leap forward for the lunatics of Hong Kong. Still, the Mental Hospital (as it was renamed) was a grim place. As Dr. Wai Hoi Lo observed, "I

joined the Government mental health service as a medical officer in July 1959 and I found the hospital to be shabby and crowded. At night, tatami mats were placed in the day room and dining room for patient to sleep on, and during the daytime patients had to walk in a small garden allowing the day room to be used for electroconvulsive therapy and other treatments." (W. H. Lo, "A Century (1885–1985) of Development of Psychiatric Services in Hong Kong—with Special Reference to Personal Experience," *Hong Kong Journal of Psychiatry*, 2003; 13(4), p. 22.)

50. E. G. Pryor, "The Great Plague of Hong Kong," *Journal of the Hong Kong Branch of the Royal Asiatic Society*, 1975, vol. 15, p. 62.

51. Ibid., p. 65.

52. Ibid., p. 63.

53. Ibid., pp. 68–69.

54. Pow Meng Yap, "Ideas of Mental Health and Disorder in Hong Kong and Their Practical Influence," *Elixir*, 1967, No. 1; p. 26.

55. Ted Kaptchuk and Michael Croucher, *The Healing Arts: Exploring Medical Ways of the World* (New York: Summit Books, 1987), p. 131.

56. While admitting at the outset that no one knew exactly what *latah* was or what caused it, Yap took on the syndrome with the knowledge of an insider and the eyes of an outsider. *Latah* was found mostly among older women in Malaysia, where Yap was born. When startled, they seemed to lose control of their speech and actions, helplessly imitating those around them as if their own self had disintegrated. Often this was accompanied with profanity. Yap noted that in interviewing one subject, "Occasionally she would interject 'nonok' (vagina), and on one or two occasions made as if to touch the examiner's genitals." In his paper, "The Latah Reaction: Its Pathodynamics and Nosological Position" (*The Journal of Mental Science*, October 1952; vol. XCVIII, no. 413, pp. 33, 516–64), he kept a cool tone, but the paper seethed

with impatience at how *latah* had been considered a "primitive hysteria" found among people with undeveloped personalities who were unable to control their urges. In contrast, Yap tried to see the condition from within Malay culture. "It is difficult to convey to someone who has not actually been to Malaya an adequate idea of the prevailing manners and customs of the different classes of people," he wrote. "They are by no means 'primitive' and indeed an ever larger number of them are being drawn into the modern world culture of radios, newspapers, nationalism and economic competition." This, he suspected, was causing a decline in *latah*. Two things Yap noticed were noteworthy. The first was that many sufferers had "played" at being *latah* when they were children. They knew was it was, what it looked like, and what you did when you had it. Perhaps this "conscious imitation of *latah* in childhood," was "later 'stamped in' by 'shock' as the cause of their illness." At the same time he observed "that Chinese persons never show the reaction unless they have been brought up from childhood in a basically Malay cultural *milieu*." Likewise, "Japanese children never succumbed to *imu* [a similar condition] unless they were brought up from childhood by Ainu parents. These facts emphasize that the immediate social and cultural environment of the subjects are of great significance in the aetiology." In other words, culture was a key factor that precipitated *latah*. But what was it about the culture? Where in the culture could the cause of *latah* be found? Yap said future research should include "investigations in into the myths, folk beliefs, proverbs, literature and drama (and in the case of the Malays also perhaps the cinema) of these ethnic groups in order to elucidate group-attitudes toward fear, violence, heroism and conquest" (ibid.). His instinct was correct. He didn't arrive there, but I believe he was going in the right direction—toward the stories they told and the scripts they performed.

57. Pow Meng Yap, "Cultural Bias in Psychiatry and Mental Health,"
    Australian and New Zealand Journal of Psychiatry, 1968, 2, p. 13.

58. It's interesting to note how many epidemics there were in the
    region at the same time: in Singapore (1967), Guangzhou (1967),
    Hong Kong (1967), and on Hainan (1966). Certainly 1967 was a
    year of change worldwide, but to have so much genital anxiety is
    striking. One possible factor mentioned to me in Singapore was
    the massacre of between 500,000 and 1,000,000 Chinese in Indo-
    nesia under the dictator Suharto (Marylyn Berger, "Suharto Dies
    at 86; Indonesian Dictator Brought Order and Bloodshed," New
    York Times, January 28, 2008). Tseng et al. (Wen-Shing Tseng,
    Mo Kan-Ming, et al., "Koro Epidemics in Guangdong, China: A
    Questionnaire Survey," The Journal of Nervous and Mental Disease,
    1992, 180, p. 122) report that past epidemics on Hainan were each
    preceded by major social upheaval: In 1952, it was the Land Reform
    and redistribution of property. In 1966, it was the Cultural Revo-
    lution. In 1974, there was an epidemic of encephalitis. This is also
    one of Wolfgang Jilek's theories: That sociocultural stress mani-
    fests in these sorts of epidemics. In Li Jie's paper on the 2004 epi-
    demic in Fuhu, the eighty-year-old local healer attributed a 1963
    epidemic to the "Great Leap Movement [sic], which demanded
    that people work hard to promote production," and brought "an
    'evil wind' that intruded into people's bodies." What, then, of the
    1984–85 Hainan epidemic? One possible source of anxiety was
    the fact that Hainan was becoming independent from Guangdong
    Province, starting in 1984, when it became its own special admin-
    istrative region, through 1988, when it officially became Hainan
    Province and a "Special Economic Zone." This is speculation on
    my part, but the relationship between China and Hainan has been
    a complicated one for more than two thousand years.

59. After we finish the interview, Dr. Wai took me and his colleague—a
    younger psychiatrist whose wife practiced traditional Chinese

Medicine—to a restaurant across the street. We ate pickled pea-
nuts, freshwater river shrimp, etc. Then at one point, a woman
in a bright pink dress came in and sat down. "Do you know who
that is?" he asked. I said I didn't. It was Margaret Chan, the direc-
tor-general of the World Health Organization. After a few minutes,
he excused himself and walked over to her table and said hello.

Chapter 5: Savage Minds

60. Laurence Kirmayer, "Cultural Psychiatry in Historical Perspective," in *Textbook of Cultural Psychiatry* (Cambridge: Cambridge
University Press, 2007). p. 8.

61. Raymond Williams, *Keywords: A Vocabulary of Culture and Society*
(New York: Oxford University Press, 1976, 1987), p. 90.

62. Ibid., p. 90.

63. Peter Melville Logan, "On Culture: Edward B. Tylor's Primitive Culture, 1871," in *BRANCH: Britain, Representation and Nineteenth-
Century History*, ed. Dino Franco Felluga. Extension of Romanticism
and Victorianism on the Net. Web. (Accessed 4.15.14.)

64. George Stocking, *Victorian Anthropology* (New York: The Free
Press, 1987), p. 157.

65. Ibid.

66. Edward Burnett Tylor, *The Origins of Culture: Part I of Primitive
Culture* (New York: J. P. Putnam's Sons, 1871), p. 1.

67. This attitude remains pervasive in modern times and you can hear
shades of it in news coverage almost every day. In 1961, in the
early days of the Peace Corps, it even caused an international incident in when Margery Michelmore, one of the first volunteers in
Nigeria, wrote a postcard to her boyfriend complaining that "we
were not prepared for the squalor and absolutely primitive living
condition rampant both in the city and in the bush." Primitive
as they were, Nigerian students did have a mimeograph machine,
which they used to copy the postcard and distribute it across the

campus in Ibadan, causing protests and demands for the Peace Corps to be thrown out of the country. John Updike wrote about the incident in *The New Yorker* and Eisenhower used it as evidence of Kennedy's "juvenile experiment." Eventually the communists were blamed. The incident blew over and a few years later became a musical that ran on Broadway. (Stanley Meisler, *When the World Calls: The Inside Story of the Peace Corps and Its First Fifty Years* (Boston: Beacon Press, 2011), pp 37–42.)

68. Edward Burnett Tylor, *The Origins of Culture: Part II of Primitive Culture* (New York: J. P. Putnam's Sons, 1871), p. 453.

69. Ludger Müller-Wille and William Barr, *Franz Boas Among the Inuit of Baffin Island, 1883–1884: Journals and Letters* (Toronto: University of Toronto Press, 1998), pp. 12–15.

70. Quoted from George Stocking's *Observers Observed: Essays on Ethnographic Fieldwork* (Madison: University of Wisconsin Press, 1985), p. 33, from Boas entry on December 23, titled "December 23, Anarnitung."

71. Franz Boas, *Kwakiutl Tales Volume II* (New York: Columbia University Press, 1910).

72. Alfred Kroeber and Clyde Kluckhohn, *Culture: A Critical Review of Concepts and Definitions* (New York, Vintage Books, 1952).

Chapter 6: Bad Buns

73. Paul Ngui, "The *Koro* Epidemic in Singapore," *Australia New Zealand Journal of Psychiatry*, 1969, 3, p. 263.

74. Chong Tong Mun, "Epidemic *Koro* in Singapore," *British Medical Journal*, March 9, 1968, p. 641.

75. *Koro* Study Team, "The *Koro* 'Epidemic' in Singapore," *Singapore Medical Journal*, December 1969, 10, No. 4, pp. 234–35.

76. Ibid., p. 236.

77. Gwee Ah Leng, "*Koro*: Its Origin and Nature as a Disease Entity," *Singapore Medical Journal*, March 1968, vol. 9, no. 1, p. 3.

78. Hilary Evans and Robert E. Bartholomew, Outbreak! The Encyclopedia of Extraordinary Social Behavior (San Antonio: Anomalist Books, 2009), p. 195.

79. Ngui, 1969, p. 265.

80. *Koro* Study Team, 1969, p. 237.

81. Ngui, 1969, p. 266.

82. When I contacted Ngui to revisit our conversation, he wanted to correct something he'd said earlier, when he mentioned that *latah* sufferer shouted things like "fuck you" or "vagina." To me, this seemed consistent with what I'd read elsewhere, including Pow Meng Yap's 1952 paper in which he reported old *latah* women saying things like "nonok" (vagina) and "puki" (pussy) and "butol" (penis). Perhaps he felt this reflected badly on his culture. Nonetheless, I'll include Ngui's follow-up here, since he is one of the few people I talked to who had personal experience with it. He writes: *"Dear Frank. I would like to correct the impression that the swear word FU or vagina were commonly uttered by persons suffering from* latah *reaction. The F word would be regarded as too vulgar and crude word to be acceptable by the Peranakans. The* latah *reaction is a startle reaction induced by a sudden loud noise such as a loud clap behind the head, or a sudden poke in the ribs of a person suffering from* latah. *The* latah *person would give out a loud scream in surprise and fear for his safety as if he was attacked. He would scream out phrases repeatedly with alliteration. e.g. 'Oh my God! Oh my God!' . . . Oh my God!' . . . Oh my God!' or 'Alamak' 'Allah Mak' i.e., 'Mother of God.' He would continue repeating these phrases non-stop, and continuously with further loud claps behind him or from further digs in his ribs. Other common phrases used were 'Damn it! Damn it!,' 'Bad luck,' 'Bad luck, it's broken!' 'Broken!' . . . 'Broken!' . . . repeatedly. The audience would roar with laughter bemused by the desperate antics of the* latah *sufferer to free himself from his 'tormentors.' All this was carried out in fun, and would on occasions only end hours later*

with latah *person completely fatigued and exhausted. I would like to qualify that as a psychiatrist I personally have not come across a case of* latah *in my practice.* Latah *is a culture-bound syndrome peculiar to the Peranankans and the Malay culture. It is not seen among the Chinese from mainland China who settled in Malaysia and Singapore.*"

83. I learned this on a boat tour of the Singapore River, where the shores were lined with beefy Westerners drinking Heinekens and Jagerbombs. On the video monitor, a breathless narrator told us about Singapore's "gritty past, vibrant present, and exciting future." At one point, there was shouting from the front of the boat and I saw the guide chasie several German teenagers off the bow. Afterward, their father complained loudly that his children were "very angry," they couldn't sit on the front of the boat. The guide shrugged and looked defeated.

84. The science fiction writer William Gibson called it "Disneyland with the Death Penalty," in *Wired Magazine*. I could see why: its gritty past is now preserved like a dead thing for visitors to see, or a ride to take.

85. Interestingly, Singapore was divided between immigrants from Hokkien and Teochow and Canton until the 1950s when a major "reurbanization" effort tried to integrate the city's ethnicities, including those from China.

86. That same week, a headline in the *Malay Mail* read: "Two killed, two injured as man runs amok."

Chapter 7: American Maladies

87. Usually the implication of this sort of statement is that if PMS is "socially constructed," meaning that it is not real. This is not what I'm saying. If you were to tell a victim of penis theft in Nigeria that he was suffering from a cultural syndrome or that his penis theft was caused by his belief in it, his reaction would be the same anger and disbelief as when you tell an American woman PMS is a

cultural syndrome (more specifically, a cultural idiom of distress). This reaction comes from questioning not only a belief, but the very forces holding a person's world together, in these cases meaning biochemistry and magic. It's like telling a Christian there's no God or telling Richard Dawkins there is one.

88. Mari Rodin, "The Social Construction of Prementrual Syndrome," *Social Science and Medicine*, 1992, vol. 35. no. 1, p. 50.

89. Ian Hacking, *Mad Travelers: Reflections on the Reality of Transient Mental Illness* (Charlottesville: University Press of Virginia, 1998), p. 72.

90. Robert T. Frank, "The Hormonal Basis of Premenstrual Tension," *Archives of Neurological Psychiatry*, 1931, 26, pp. 1053–57.

91. Katharina Dalton and Raymond Greene, "The Premenstrual Syndrome," *British Medical Journal*, 1953, 1, p. 1007–14.

92. Joan C. Chrisler and Paula Caplan, "The Strange Case of Dr. Jekyll and Ms. Hyde: How PMS Became a Cultural Phenomenon and a Psychiatric Disorder," *Annual Review of Sex Research*, 2002, 13:1, p. 276.

93. Loes Knaapen and George Weisz, "The Biomedical Standardization of Premenstrual Syndrome," *Studies in History and Philosophy of Biological and Biomedical Sciences*, 2008, 39, p. 125.

94. Ibid., p. 126.

95. Ibid. The media also played a role in this shift with news stories like "Coping with Eve's Curse" and "The Taming of the Shrew Inside of You," among others, that talked about how "hormonal shifts can turn ordinary women into monsters" (Chrisler and Caplan, 2002, p. 286).

96. Another complicating factor are pharmaceuticals. In 2000, the company Eli Lilly introduced a drug for PMDD called Sarafem, which was the same drug (fluoxetine) as Prozac, just colored pink instead of green and packaged and marketed differently. As one writer noted, "The side effects of Fluoxetine are: insomnia, anxiety, nervousness, and somnolence. These are similar, if not identical,

to some of the symptoms of PMDD" (healthpsych.psy.vanderbilt. edu/PMDD_and_Sarafem.htm).

97. The *DSM-5* states, paradoxically: "Premenstrual dysphoric disorder is not a culture-bound syndrome and has been observed in individuals in the United States, Europe, India, and Asia. It is unclear as to whether rates differ by race. Nevertheless, frequency, intensity, and expressivity of symptoms and help-seeking patterns may be significantly influenced by cultural factors" (American Psychiatric Association, *Diagnostic and Statistical Manual of Mental Disorders, 5th Edition* [Arlington, VA: American Psychiatric Publishing, 2013, p. 173]).

98. In other cultures, menstruation has a more positive meaning and is described in positive terms. It's not thought of as a debilitating condition that needs medical treatment. For example, on the island of Wogeo, Papua New Guinea, menstruation is seen as so powerful and cleansing that men are expected to menstruate too. They do this by walking into the ocean naked, inducing an erection, pushing the foreskin back, then slicing at the glans on either side with the claw of a crab. When the bleeding stops and the ocean water around the man is clear, he returns to shore, wraps his penis in medicinal leaves, and is considered cleansed. The same word is used for male and female menstruation. (Ian Hogbin, *The Island of Menstruating Men: Religion in Wogeo, New Guinea* [Prospect Heights, IL: Waveband Press, 1996], pp. 88–89). According to Chrisler and Caplan, "World Health Organization surveys indicate that menstrual cycle-related complaints (except cramps) are most likely to be reported by women who live in Western Europe, Australia, and North America. Data collected from women in Hong Kong and mainland China indicate that the most commonly reported premenstrual symptoms are fatigue, water retention, pain, and increased sensitivity to cold. American women do not report cold sensitivity and Chinese women rarely

report negative affect" (Chrisler and Caplan, 2002, p. 285). On a related note, menopause also changes across cultures. Margaret Lock has investigated this and found wide variation. In Massachusetts, 35 percent of women experienced hot flashes and 10 percent had night sweats. In Japan, the rates were 10 percent and 4 percent. Essentially, as a medical condition menopause did not exist in Japan. Likewise, rates were low or nonexistent among Mayan Indians, North Africans, and Israelis, while they were higher in people from North America, Europe, and Varanasi in India (cited in Moerman, 2002, pp. 74–75; see Margaret Lock and Patricia Kaufert, "Menopause, Local Biologies, and Cultures of Aging," *American Journal of Human Biology*, 2001, 13, pp. 494–504).

99.   Tamara Kayali Browne, "Is Premenstrual Dysphoric Disorder Really a Disorder?" *Journal of Bioethical Inquiry*, June 2015, vol. 12, iss. 2, p. 6.

100. As Thomas Johnson wrote in his paper, "Premenstrual Syndrome as a Western Culture-Specific Disorder," "We strive to discover the biological 'reality' of PMS, for example, without examining the cultural forces which are attendant in the process of creating that reality. We are willing to see culture-bound syndromes in other cultures when we cannot readily understand their symptom complexes in biomedical terms. Even though there are those who strive to find congruence between bizarre symptom complexes in other cultures and Western biomedical disease entities, there has been an implication that such syndromes are 'not real.' Yet we unquestioningly treat our own problematic syndromes, such as PMS, as 'real,' striving constantly to find physiological correlates of symptoms" (Thomas Johnson, "Premenstrual Syndrome as a Western Culture-Specific Disorder," *Culture, Medicine and Psychiatry*, 1987, 11, p. 347). Others have made similar observations. "The dominance of PMS discourse was evidenced by the fact that we had difficulty finding participants who did not experience PMS," wrote

researchers Lisa Cosgrove and Bethany Riddle in 2008. They found (as had others) that women who endorsed traditional gender roles experienced more menstrual distress. "One of the most striking results," they wrote, "was that PMS discourse has gained such cultural currency that women often expect to have PMS" (Lisa Cosgrove and Bethany Riddle, "Constructions of Femininity and Experiences of Menstrual Distress," *Women & Health* 2003, 38:3, pp. 37–58). Another study found that patients "firmly believed that PMS is biologically based, and they rejected situational attributions for their distress" (Chrisler and Caplan, 2002, p. 287). In a land-mark experiment, Diane Ruble found that women who were misled to believe they were premenstrual experienced more symptoms of PMS than those who were actually premenstrual, but who were misled to believe they were not (Jeanne Brooks, Diane Ruble, and Anne Claris, "College Women's Attitudes and Expectations Con-cerning Menstrual-Related Changes," *Psychosomatic Medicine*, Sep-tember–October 1977, vol. 39, no. 5, pp. 288–98). None of which is to say that these symptoms aren't real. Rather, again, that they are caused by our culture, by our understanding of the body, and by our expectations of the experience as we will see in Chapter 9.

101. Lynn Payer, *Medicine and Culture* (New York, Owl Books, 1996), p. 15.

102. Other unusual conditions: In Italy, you might come down with the "cervicale," or "cervical," for which there is no equivalent in any other language (Dany Mitzman, "How to Avoid Getting 'Hit by Air' in Italy," *BBC Magazine*, December 3, 2011). In France, a phar-macist will be familiar with "heavy legs" and can give you grape-seed oil to rub between your ankles and knees (Emma Jane Kirby, "A Curiously French Complaint," *From Our Own Correspondent*, *BBC News*, December 13, 2008: news.bbc.co.uk/go/pr/fr/-/2/hi /programmes/from_our_own_correspondent/7779126.stm).

103. As Payer wrote, "Anything that cannot fit into the machine model

of the body, or be quantified, is often denied not only quantification, but even existence" (ibid., p. 151).

104. Allard Dembe, *Occupation and Disease: How Social Factors Affect the Conception of Work-Related Disorders* (New Haven: Yale University Press, 1996), p. 33.

105. Ibid., pp. 36–39.

106. Ibid., p. 88.

107. Ibid., p. 93.

108. From the National Institute of Mental Health Directors Blog, retrieved November 7, 2014: www.nimh.nih.gov/about/director /2013/transforming-diagnosis.shtml.

109. Interview with the author, July 2013.

110. Roberto Lewis-Fernandez, Devon Hinton, et al., "Review: Culture and the Anxiety Disorders: Recommendations for the *DSM-V*," *Depression and Anxiety*, 2009, 0, pp. 1–18.

111. Jeanne Tsai and Yulia Chentsova Dutton, "Understanding Depression Across Cultures," in *Handbook of Depression*, edited by Ian Gotlib and Constance L. Hammen (New York: Guildford Press, 2002), p. 471.

112. Ibid., p. 472.

113. Yulia Chentsova Dutton, Andrew Ryder, Jeanne Tsai, "Understanding Depression across Cultural Contexts," in Ian Gotlib and Constance L. Hammen, eds., *Handbook of Depression*, 3rd ed. (New York: Guildford Press, 2014), p. 340.

114. Evelyn Bromet, Laura Helena Andrade, et al., "Cross-national Epidemiology of *DSM-IV* Major Depressive Episode," *BMC Medicine*, 2011, 9, p. 90.

115. Uriel Halbreich and Sandhya Karkun, "Cross-cultural and Social Diversity of Prevalence of Postpartum Depression and Depressive Symptoms," *Journal of Affective Disorders*, 2006, pp. 97–111.

116. In Hopi, there isn't a single word for "depression." Rather, it's divided into worry sickness, unhappiness; heartbreak, "drunken-

like craziness" and "turning one's face to the wall" (Spero Manson et al., "Depressive Experience in American Indian Communities: A Challenge for Psychiatric Theory and Diagnosis," in *Culture and Depression: Studies in the Anthropology and Cross Cultural Psychiatry of Affect and Disorder* [Berkeley: University of California Press, 1985], pp. 336–39). In Yoruba, the same word is used for depression, anxiety, anger, and sadness. And in Japanese, the word "jodo," translated as "emotion," can also mean lucky, motivated, and calculating (Christopher Dowrick, *Beyond Depression: A New Approach to Understanding and Management,* 2nd Edition [Oxford: Oxford University Press, 2009], p. 131). The important question this raises is whether our particular definition, and understanding, of "depression" shapes our experience of it. According to a strict biomedical model, that kind of causal flow is impossible. According to much other evidence, it's probable.

117. Ethan Watters's *Crazy Like Us: The Globalization of the American Psyche* (New York: The Free Press, 2010), p. 137. See also J. Leff, N. Sartorius, et al., "The International Pilot Study of Schizophrenia: Five-Year Follow-Up Findings," *Psychological Medicine*, 1992, 22, pp. 131–45.

118. "Cross-National Comparisons of the Prevalences and Correlates of Mental Disorders," *Bulletin of the World Health Organization*, Geneva, January 2000, vol. 78, no. 4: dx.doi.org/10.1590/S0042-96862000000400003.

119. Sadly, the growing belief that mental diseases are physical diseases may actually increase the stigma of those who are mentally ill. In his book, *Crazy Like Us*, Ethan Watters writes: "The logic seemed unassailable: once people believed that the symptoms of mental illnesses such as schizophrenia were not the choice of the individual and did not spring from supernatural forces, the sufferer would be protected from blame . . . It turns out that those who adopted the biomedical and genetic beliefs about mental illness

were most often those who wanted less contact with the mentally ill and thought of them as dangerous and unpredictable" (Watters, 2010, pp. 172–73).

120. Christopher Dowrick, "Depression as a Culture-bound Syndrome: Implications for Primary Care," *British Journal of General Practice*, May 2013, pp. 229–30.

121. University of Michigan, "Brooding Russians: Less Distressed than Americans," *ScienceDaily*, July 14, 2010: www.sciencedaily.com /releases/2010/07/100713122844.htm.

122. Charles C. Hughes, "The Glossary of 'Culture-Bound Syndromes' in *DSM-IV*: A Critique," *Transcultural Psychiatry*, September 1998, vol. 35, no. 3, pp. 417–18.

123. In the *DSM-5*, which came out in 2013, borders between culture and biology became slightly more porous. The term "culture-bound syndromes" has been replaced by the less restrictive term "cultural syndromes" and the more useful "cultural concepts of distress." The text notes, "Like culture and the *DSM* itself, cultural concepts may change over time in response to both local and global influences," and that "all forms of distress are locally shaped, including the *DSM* disorders." This is a striking admission and represents a step away from a reductionist biomedical model—from the idea that mental illnesses are really just physical illnesses. This seems to be a grudging acceptance of the fast that culture matters. (*Diagnostic and Statistical Manual of Mental Disorders*, 5th ed. [Washington, D.C.: American Psychiatric Publishing, 2013], p. 758). A number of syndromes now have a short paragraph on "Culture-related diagnostic issues," and there is also an extensive "Cultural Formulation Interview," to help patients explain their cultural background to psychiatrists.

124. Interview with the author, July 2013.

Chapter 8: Mingling Medicine

125. *Encyclopedia Britannica* (Chicago: Encyclopedia Britannica, 1968), vol. 4, p. 808.

126. I could not find this reference. It is, however, a crazy construction.

127. *Guangzhou Travel Guide/Map*, 2013.

128. Dade Road General Hospital History: www.gdhtcm.com/sitecn /lsyg/index.html.

129. Hospital Introduction, Guangdong Kyorin first—advance the Hospital of Guangdong Province: www.gdhtcm.com/sitecn/yyjs/index .html. Via Google Translate.

130. Lulu Zhang and Yuping Ning, "Guangzhou Psychiatric Hospital: The Oldest Psychiatric Hospital in China," *Psychiatry* (Edgemont), 2010, 7(6), pp. 53–54.

131. Dr. Li Jie, "*Koro* Endemic Among School Children in Guangdong, China," *World Cultural Psychiatry Research Review*, December 2010, pp. 102–105.

132. This is a technique that uses "warm" materials, or moxa, to redirect blood and qi flow.

133. This was quite high. A 1993 study found that the knowledge of *suo yang* was the same in three distant parts of China, but the *fear* of it was not: In the northern province of Jilin, only 10 percent of people believed *koro* was "a dangerous condition needing immediate help." In Taiwan, 20 percent of the people did. In Guangdong province (where Fuhu was located), 45 percent of people did (W. S. Tseng, K. M. Mo, G. Q. Chen, L. X. Li, R. G. Wen, and T. S. Liu, "Social Psychiatry and Epidemic Koro: [4] Regional Comparison of Shuoyang Belief" *[Chinese] Chinese Mental Health Journal*, 7: 38–40, 1993, cited in Jie, 2010). "This illustrated," Li wrote, "that, beyond knowledge, belief in *koro* is more crucial to the occurrence of a *koro* attack and *koro* epidemic" (Li, 2010, p. 103).

134. There are some fascinating photos at this site: emsique.blogspot .com/2013/04/french-colonial-zhanjiang.html.

Chapter 9: Strange Loops

135. In the past, speaking in tongues, also known as "glossolalia," was thought to be the product of weak, primitive, or ignorant minds. In the mid-twentieth century, there was debate among medical professionals about whether it should be considered a pathology—an illness. But in her 1972 book, *Speaking in Tongues: Cross-Cultural Study of Glossolalia* (Chicago: University of Chicago Press), Felicitas Goodman concluded that it wasn't abnormal. Rather, it was a disassociative state like religious trance states across the world, including those of the Hungarian taltoskok shamans, Tibetan state oracles, and Amerindian medicine men. Goodman also found that glossolalia was not really a spontaneous behavior, but a learned one. "In many cases, of course, what looks like a spontaneous occurrence is not really that. A powerful conditioning factor is present . . . This factor, mentioned before, is cultural expectation" (ibid., p. 71). She noted that this expectation is transmitted "either by way of demonstration or word of mouth," and that "in one way or another most supplicants receive some preliminary information concerning such behavior, what happens, and how it appears to the onlooker" (ibid., p. 73). In other words, the script is learned, regardless of what neurological/spiritual doors it opens. Recent neuroimaging research has further shown that glossolalia is associated with specific neurological patterns (Andrew Newberg, Nancy Wintering, et al., "The Measurement of Regional Cerebral Blood Flow During Glossolalia: A Preliminary SPECT Study," *Psychiatry Research: Neuroimaging*, 2006, 148, pp. 67–71) and that it is a state that can be learned and induced, and which may play a role in reducing stress (Christopher Lynn, Jason Paris, et al., "Salivary Alpha-Amylase and Cortisol Among Pentecostals on a Worship and Nonworship Day," *American Journal of Human Biology*, November–December, 2010, 22[6], pp. 819–22). In fact, researchers have found that 80 percent people who practice "glos-

solalia" have "greater emotional stability and less neuroticism" than those who don't. Other studies have found that glossolalia has a variety of health benefits and no negative effects (Newberg, 2006, p. 70). One EEG study found that in a particular patient, glossolalia produced an anomalous spike in her right temporal lobe activity that caused her left arm to twitch when she spoke in tongues, but at no other time (R. R. Reeves, S. Kose, and A. Abubakr, "Temporal Lobe Discharges and Glossolalia," *Neurocase*, April 2014, 20(2), pp. 236–40). It was, as the neuroscience blogger Neuroskeptic observed, "a reminder that brain activity can be *caused by* behaviour, as well as causing it" (Neuroskeptic, "The Brain, Speaking in Tongues?" Discovermagazine.com, April 7, 2013: blogs.discovermagazine.com/neuroskeptic/2013/04/07/the-brain-speaking-in-tongues/#.VnCOzMqtjzM).

136. Yap, 1951, pp. 321–22.

137. Walter Cannon, "Voodoo Death," *American Anthropologist*, 1942, 44, pp. 169–81.

138. Ibid., p. 187.

139. A few examples: In 1972, a twenty-year-old Honduran paraplegic named Moisses Quijada came to the Mayo Hospital, where he stayed for a year attempting to overcome a "voodoo-like belief in his native village that robs cripples of their will to live." He died several months after returning home (Wintrob, 1973, p. 319). In 1936 in Hong Kong, a twenty-one-year-old woman delivered her first child at Tsan Yuk Maternity Hospital. The delivery was normal, but doctors were puzzled because the mother refused to talk or eat or nurse her baby. On the sixth day, she broke her silence and told one of the nurses that she was going to die. Outside the hospital, before admission, she had stopped at a fortune teller's booth and was told she would die on the sixth day. Later that day, she did. "[A]t the necropsy, nothing could be found to account for her death" (W.C.W. Nixon, "Scared to Death?" *British Medical*

Journal, September 18, 1965, pp. 700–701). "Big Paddy" was an aboriginal tracker for the police in a small, isolated West Australian town who was out on a patrol looking for a murder suspect in 1968 when they surprised the tribe thought to be responsible. The offending tribe's witch doctor cursed the tracking crew and afterward Big Paddy was deeply affected. He spoke little and seemed cut off from his surrounding. "He would not look at his White companion, but with the greatest difficulty he could eat a little. Despite all efforts, he became weaker and died within a few weeks" (G. W. Milton, "Self-Willed Death or the Bone-Pointing Syndrome," *Lancet*, June, 23, 1973, p. 1435). In Labrador, Canada, in 1965, a forty-three-year-old woman was admitted to North West River Hospital. She was "apparently healthy," but she'd had "severe stress incontinence" for several months. She was found to have a cystocele on her urethrocele, and underwent a short, simple operation to remove it. Afterward, she left to go to the theater, but came back an hour later complaining of severe pain and had low blood pressure. Doctors tried to relieve both conditions but she gradually got worse, fell into a coma, and died. The doctors later learned that she had been told by a fortune teller at age five that she would die when she was forty-three, and had repeatedly mentioned this to her daughter (A. R. Elkington, P. R. Steele, and D. D. Yun, "Scared to Death?" *British Medical Journal*, August 7, 1965, pp. 363–64). A 1977 paper recounted how a healthy, thirty-three-year-old man was admitted to University of Arkansas for Medical Services' neurology unit, after having had seizures and hallucinations and becoming withdrawn from his family. The doctors who examined him said, "All neurological findings, including a brain scan, proved normal." Two weeks later, he was dead. Afterward, the man's wife told them he had been seeing a "two-headed," a woman who healed and cast spells through "hoodoo," or "rootwork," the religion brought from West Africa by slaves and mixed with Christianity and Native American herbalism. Somehow the man had angered the two-headed and she'd cursed him (Kenneth Golden, "Voodoo in a General Hospital," *American Journal of Psychiatry*, December 1977, 134:12, pp. 1425–27). However, these curses only seem to work if one believes in their power. As Kenneth Golden wrote, "A number of prerequisites to the success of a curse or hex appear wherever in the world they are found: the victim must believe in the power of the person who administers the curse and must either know or at least suspect that a hex has been placed" (Golden, 1977, p. 1426). A case in point: In 2008, a Hindu fakir named Pandit Surender Sharma boasted on television that he could kill another man with his spiritual power. The head of the Indian Rationalist Society, Sanal Edamaruku, heard this and challenged Sharma to take his life live on television. For several hours, the two of them stood together while Sharma attempted to spiritually assassinate Edamaruku. The holy many clearly believed in his own power. Edamaruku clearly did not. If he had, he might have been in trouble. But in the end, Edamaruku made Sharma look like a fraud, even though neither of them really understood the powers they were trafficking in (Sanal Edamaruku, "The Night a Guru Tried to Kill Me on TV," *The Guardian*, March 23, 2010: www.theguardian.com/commentisfree/belief/2010/mar/23/surender-sharma-tv-ritual-edamaruku). In 2014, Edamaruku had to flee the country to escape a blasphemy trial after investigating a dripping statue of Jesus Christ, onto which he found the water was overflowing from a nearby toilet (Samanthi Dissanayake, "The Indian Miracle-Buster Stuck in Finland," *BBC News*, June 3, 2014: www.bbc.com/news/magazine-26815298).

140. Ronald Wintrob, "The Influence of Others: Witchcraft and Rootwork as Explanations of Behavior Distrubances," *The Journal of Nervous and Mental Disease*, 1973, vol. 156, no. 5, pp. 322–23.

141. Sandford Cohen, "Voodoo Death, the Stress Response, and

AIDS," *Psychological, Neuropsychiatric and Substance Abuse Aspects of AIDS (Advances in Biochemical Psychopharmacology)*, 1988, vol. 44, p. 95.

142. Shelley Adler, *Sleep Paralysis: Night-mares, Nocebos and the Mind-Body Connection* (New Brunswick: Rutgers University Press, 2011), p. 120.

143. Elaine Eaker, Joan Pinsky, and William Castelli, "Myocardial Infarction and Coronary Death Among Women: Psychosocial Predictors from a Twenty-Year Follow-Up of Women in the Framingham Study," *American Journal of Epidemiology*, 1992; 135(8): pp. 854–64.

144. Becca Levy, Martin Slade, et al., "Longevity Increased by Positive Self-Perceptions of Aging," *Journal of Personality and Social Psychology*, 2002, vol. 83, no. 2, pp. 261–70.

145. D. P. Phillips, T. E. Ruth, and L. M. Wagner, "Psychology and Survival," *Lancet*, 342, 1993 (8880), pp. 1142–45. Cited in Daniel Moerman's *Meaning, Medicine and the "Placebo Effect,"* (Cambridge: Cambridge University Press, 2002), p. 78.

146. David Phillips, George Liu, et al., *"The Hound of the Baskervilles* Effect: Natural Experiment on the Influence of Psychological Stress on Timing of Death," *British Medical Journal*, December 22–29, 2001, vol. 323, pp. 1443–46.

147. Adler, 2011, p. 94.

148. Ibid., pp. 14–16.

149. Ibid., p. 98.

150. Ibid., p. 129.

151. Ibid., p. 101.

152. Jon Levine, Newton Gordon, and Howard Fields, "The Mechanism of Placebo Analgesia," *Lancet*, 1978, 312 (98091): pp. 654–57. Cited in Moerman, 2002, pp. 103–104. Also in Frank Miller, Luana Collaca, Robert Crouch and Ted Kaptchuk, *The Placebo Reader* (Baltimore: Johns Hopkins University Press, 2013), p. 106.

153. Fabrizio Benedetti, Elisa Carlino, Antonella Pollo, "Hidden Administration of Drugs," *Clinical Pharmacology and Therapeutics*, November 2011, vol. 90, no. 5, pp. 652–53.

154. Fabrizio Benedetti, *The Placebo Effects: Understanding the Mechanisms in Health and Disease, 2nd edition* (Oxford: Oxford University Press, 2014), pp. 61–63 and pp. 75–80. Ted Kaptchuk has also focused on the importance of the healing ritual, which seems to tap some primal power to activate our healing systems—in the modern context, going to the doctor's office can serve such a purpose. It's also important to note is the fact that, as Benedetti writes, "There is not a single mechanism of the placebo effect and not a single placebo effect—but many" (Benedetti, 2014, pp. 43–44).

155. Slavenka Kam-Hansen, Moshe Jakubowski, Ted Kaptchuk et al., "Altered Placebo and Drug Labeling Changes the Outcome of Episodic Migraine Attacks," *Science Translational Medicine*, 2014, 6, 218ra5.

156. J. Bruce Moseley, Kimberly O'Malley, et al., "A Controlled Trial of Arthroscopic Surgery for Osteoarthritis of the Knee," *New England Journal of Medicine*, July 11, 2002, vol. 347, no. 2, pp. 81–88. See also Susan Mayor, "Arthroscopic Meniscal Tear Surgery Is No Better Than Sham Surgery, Study Shows," *British Medical Journal*, January 3, 2014, 348:g4. For a look at the placebo results across different surgeries, see Karolina Wartolowska, Andrew Judge, et al., "Use of Placebo Controls in the Evaluation of Surgery: Systematic Review," *British Medical Journal*, May 21, 2014; 348:g3253. The researchers here showed that placebo surgery was often just as effective as (or more effective than) actual surgery. The authors usually interpret this as meaning the surgeries are useless, rather than concluding that the placebo surgery can have powerful healing results. To disentangle that, both sham and actual surgeries would need to be compared to a "no treatment" group.

157. Daniel Moerman, "Examining a Powerful Healing Effect Through

a Cultural Lens, and Finding Meaning," *The Journal of Mind–Body Regulation*, vol. 1, iss. 2, p. 70.

158. Franklin G. Miller , David F. Kallmes, and Rachelle Buchbinder, "Vertebroplasty and the Placebo Response," *Radiology*, June 2011, vol. 259, no. 3, pp. 621–25.

159. John Lacey, "All Placebos Not Created Alike in a Trial of Sham Acupuncture vs. Oral Placebo Pill, Patients Experienced Greater Pain Reduction from Sham Device Than Those Receiving Placebo Pill," *Harvard Medical School Office of Public Affairs*, February 1, 2006.

160. Ted J. Kaptchuk, William B. Stason, et al., "Sham Device v Inert Pill: Randomised Controlled Trial of Two Placebo Treatments," *British Medical Journal*, February 1, 2006, Online First.

161. Avraham Schweiger and Allen Parducci, "Nocebo: The Psychologic Induction of Pain," *The Pavlovian Journal of Biological Science*, July–September, 1981, 16(3); pp. 140–43.

162. Piero Vernia et al., "Diagnosis of Lactose Intolerance and the 'Nocebo' Effect: The Role of Negative Expectations," *Digestive and Liver Disease*, 2010, 42, pp. 616–19.

163. Melinda Beck, "Power of Suggestions: When Drug Labels Make You Sick," *Wall Street Journal*, November 18, 2008, p. D1.

164. Moerman, 2002, p. 84.

165. Fabrizio Benedetti, Elisa Carlino, Antonella Pollo, "How Placebos Change the Patient's Brain," *Neuropsychopharmacology*, 2011, 36, pp. 339–54. Moerman argues that the placebo effect should actually be called the "meaning effect," while others have made the case for calling it the "care effect," based on the influence of doctors. A 1966 study showed that a mild tranquilizer called meprobamate seemed to work better than the placebo some of the time, but *only* if the doctors were solicitous, confident, and enthusiastic (Moerman, 2002, p. 37). A 2009 study by John M. Kelley looked at 289 people with irritable bowel syndrome, and divided them into three groups, one of which got no treatment, another that got sham acupuncture

with a neutral and business-like caregiver, and another that got treatment from a caregiver who was "warm and empathic" and who "used active listening skills and communicated confidence and positive expectations about the treatment." The last group had a "very large" effect, while the first two had only a "medium"-size effect (John M. Kelley and Anthony J. Limbo, "Patient and Practitioner Influences on the Placebo Effect in Irritable Bowel Syndrome," *Psychosomatic Medicine*, 2009, 71, pp. 789–97). It is possible these interactions serve to strengthen our expectations of improvement, or to trigger a sense of being needed by the group, which, in turn, ramps up the endogenous health-care system. But that is speculation on my part. Further research is needed.

166. One of Moerman's most important findings to illustrate this point is how the placebo effects vary wildly across cultures. In trials for ulcer drugs in Germany, he found an average 59 percent placebo healing rate—much higher than in neighboring Netherlands, which had a rate of 22 percent, and two times higher than the rest of the world. But in Brazil, ulcer drug trials showed a placebo healing rate of only 7 percent. This carried over into the drug itself, which had healing rates of 78 percent in Germany and 54 percent in Brazil. The drugs worked, but they worked better alongside some unknown German beliefs. These cultural differences are widespread: In America, placebo shots work better than placebo pills, but not in Europe. Pink tablets tend to make people more alert. Blue pills tend to make them less—but not in Italian men (where blue is the national soccer team's color). A study in the 1980s found that people from Italian, Irish and Hispanic cultures experienced greater pain than people from Polish, French Canadian, and old American cultures (see Moerman, 2002, Chapter 8). No one knows what these particular beliefs are, but people's understandings of the body varies wildly. As Lynn Payer points out, Germans have an entirely different idea of what the heart is. They see it as

"an organ that has a life of its own, one that pulsates in response to a number of different stimuli, including emotions" (Payer, 1996, p. 80). This leads Germans to be extremely concerned that their heart is working sufficiently. In Germany, if you have low blood pressure, you will be diagnosed with "*Herzinsuffizienz*" and given heart medication. The literal translation of that is "congestive heart failure," though what it really means is something different. Germany consumes more heart medication than any other country in the world. Americans, meanwhile, view the heart as a simple pump. We see the veins as pipes. That's why the artificial heart was developed in America: When a part wears out in your car, or your body, we believe you can get another one. The fact that the artificial heart failed would not have surprised a German doctor, who would see the heart as part of a much more complicated loop that includes thoughts, feelings, and emotions (Payer, 1996, pp. 74–100). Americans will be diagnosed with more viruses, and prescribed far more antibiotics, than people in France or Germany, because we believe in, and fear, germs. The French don't even have the phrase "germ theory of disease," only "germ theory of *transmissible* disease."

167. Richard Gracely, Ronald Dubner William Deeter, and Patricia Wolskee, "Clinicians' Expectations Influence Placebo Analgesia," *Lancet*, 1985, 325 (8419), p. 43. Also in Miller et al., *The Placebo Reader*, 2013, p. 115.

168. Abiola Keller, Kristin Litzelman, et al., "Does the Perception that Stress Affects Health Matter? The Association with Health and Mortality," *Health Psychology*, September 2012, 31(5), pp. 677–84.

169. McGonigal defines mindset as "a belief that biases how you think, feel and act" that "is usually based on a theory about how the world works" (McGonigal, 2015, p. TK).

170. Kelly McGonigal, *The Upside of Stress: Why Stress Is Good for You, and How to Get Good at It* (New York: Avery, 2015), p. 11.

171. Ibid., p. 110.

172. Ibid., pp. 9–10. Both the "threat response" and the "challenge response" increase levels of the stress hormone cortisol, which is helpful in the short term but in the long term is associated with decreased immune function and increased depression risk. The "challenge response" also increases DHEA, which counters some of the negative effects of cortisol.

173. Dana Carney, Amy Cuddy, and Andy Yap, "Power Posing: Brief Nonverbal Displays Affect Neuroendocrine Levels and Risk Tolerance," *Psychological Science*, 21(10), pp. 1363–1368.

174. Matthieu Riccard, Antoine Lutz, and Richard Davidson, "Mind of the Meditator," *Scientific American*, November 2014, p. 45.

175. Michael Gazzaniga, *Who's in Charge? Free Will and the Science of the Brain (the Gifford Lectures 2009)* (New York: Ecco, 2011), pp. 137–40.

176. Hacking, 1998, p. 7.

177. Ibid., p. 1.

178. In the late 1800s, the rise of global transport and mass tourism opened up vast new possibilities for personal travel. In the 1870s and '80s, Thomas Cook & Sons were selling 7 million tickets a year for trips through Europe and the Middle East. This, Hacking argues, was the niche that gave rise to *fugue* (ibid., pp. 27–30).

179. Ian Hacking, "Madness: Biological or Constructed," in *The Social Construction of What?* (Cambridge: Harvard University Press, 2001), pp. 109–10.

180. From the author's interview with Hinton. See also Devon E. Hinton, Vuth Pich, et al., "Khyâl Attacks: A Key Idiom of Distress Among Traumatized Cambodia Refugees," *Culture Medicine and Psychiatry*, 2010, 34, pp. 244–78.

181. Elizabeth Thao, "The Next Wave of Hmong Shamans: Sandy'Ci Moua's Story," Twin Cities Daily Planet, April 2, 2013.

Chapter 10: The Dragon's Tail

182. Edward Schafer, *Shore of Pearls* (Berkeley: University of California Press, 1970), pp. 85–86.

183. "On the Birth of a Son," translated by Arthur Waley, printed in *Poetry: A Magazine of Verse*, 1918 (edited by Harriet Monroe).

184. Schafer, 1970, p. 86

185. Demi, *Su Dungpo: Chinese Genius* (New York: Lee & Low Books Inc., 2006).

186. Lin'gao, which has historically been spelled Limkow, Linkow, Limko, or Limkao, and whose language is known to its roughly one million speakers as Ong-Be, should, according to strict pinyin rules, be spelled Lin'gao to avoid translational confusion with Ling'ao, which is the site of a nuclear power plant north of Hong Kong.

187. The Chinese businessman Charlie Soong, who came from Hainan (and whose three daughters would marry Chiang Kai-shek, Sun Yat-sen, and H. H. Kung, once China's richest man), financed a Hainanese/Chinese dictionary, but today it's impossible to find. Beyond that, there are at least ten other languages spoken on the island, including the languages of the minority Li (distantly related to Thai) and Miao (the Chinese word for *Hmong*); there is Lin'gaohua (spoken only in Lin'gao, related to Thai), Cham (a Malayo-Polynesian language from Vietnam), Cunhua (in the Thai family), Danzhouhua (formerly considered a Cantonese dialect, but now is "unclassified" Chinese and spoken only in Danzhou), the Min dialect, as well as the Junhua, Hakka, Maihua, and Danjia dialects. In more sophisticated corners, people speak Mandarin. A true linguistic landscape of Hainan, however, is very hard to compose without a working knowledge of Chinese. There is some useful English-language information at www.ethnologue.com and in these papers: Graham Thurgood, "Hainan Cham, Anong, and Eastern Cham: Three Languages, Three Social Contexts, Three Patterns of Change," *Journal of Language Contact*, 2010, VARIA

3; Graham Thurgood, "From Atonal to Tonal in Utsat (A Chamic Language of Hainan)," *Proceedings of the Eighteenth Annual Meeting of the Berkeley Linguistics Society: Special Session on the Typology of Tone Languages,* 1992; Therephan L-Thongkum, "The Tai-Kadai Peoples of Hainan Island and Their Languages," in *Essays in Tai Linguistics,* eds. M. R. Kalaya Tingsabadh and A. S. Abramson (Chulalongkorn University Press), pp. 189–204. Thanks also to Graham Thurgood for his assistance.

188. One evening I got on my rental bike, pedaled back to the Twinkle Star, then went to go find some "Hainan Chicken," which is famous from Singapore to Bangkok. Marian had explicitly forbidden this, saying, "It's disgusting! It's a half-cooked, parboiled chicken. I can't tell you how many disappointed people I've had here from Singapore." And so it was. But it passed the time.

189. Tseng et al., 1988, p. 1540.

190. Jilek, 1986, p. 278.

191. Tseng et al., 1988, p. 1541.

192. Another case Jilek recorded was a man who lived in Zhanjiang town. He was also twenty-eight years old, worked as an accountant, and had nine years of formal schooling. The attack happened after he got into bed, but couldn't fall asleep: *"It was 20 minutes past 10 p.m. I saw the window was open. I heard something jumping into my bedroom. I turned on my torch and looked all over but could not see anything, so I went to bed again. I felt something in front of me. I stretched out my hand to grab the thing, but there was nothing there. So I went out to look, but could not see anything. I felt cold, went back to bed but could not sleep. I was shivering. Suddenly I felt my genitals shrink into my abdomen. I tried to hold my penis but could not feel it any more, only very tiny. I ran out, calling the neighbors for help. A neighbor immediately set off fire crackers, rang the bell and beat the drum. Another neighbor got a fish net and threw it over me, covered me with a fish net. Then they took two chopsticks and squeezed the middle*

finger of my left hand. If one squeezes the left middle finger, according to what people said, the evil spirit will get out there. They squeezed my middle finger for an hour. Other neighbors held on to my penis with their hands. They took turns, holding it tight. All the while they also beat the drum. They hit the floor with a vegetable chopper and yelled 'Get out you evil spirits,' They also beat me under the fishnet with sandals and slippers; actually they beat the evil spirit, yelling, 'Evil spirit get out—if you stay in him, we will kill you.' I did not feel any pain. I was too afraid, I thought I would die. After one hour I felt better. There was a little bleeding on my penis from the pulling. I feel asleep, was so tired. Next morning, my penis hurt, there was some bleeding. I went to the hospital outpatient clinic. I never had any attack again, but still cannot sleep well . . . I'm still somewhat afraid at night that I might get suk-yang *again"* (Jilek, 1986, pp. 274–75).

193. Tseng et al., 1988, say "more than 2,000 persons" (p. 1540). Jilek, 1986, says, "at least 5,000 people" (p. 273).

194. Tseng et al., 1988, p. 1541.

195. Ibid.

196. Ibid.

197. Ibid., p. 1542. In a follow-up survey of victims, Tseng et al. also found that "familiarity with and belief in the *koro* concept and belief in supernatural power as the causality of disaster is fundamental for a subject to become the victim of a *koro* attack" (Tseng et al., 1992, p. 121).

Chapter 11: The Chains That Bind Us

198. Incidentally, this is not uncommon across the world. As noted above, in Italy, people keep scarves wrapped tightly around their necks to protect them from getting a *colpo d'aria* (a hit of air) (Mitzman, 2011). Tibetans also get "wind sickness" (Ronit Yoeli-Tlalim, "Tibetan 'Wind' and 'Wind' Illnesses: Towards a Multicultural Approach to Health and Illness," *Studies in History and Philosophy*

of Biological and Biomedical Sciences, December 2010, 41–540[4–7], pp. 318–324), and in Korea, papers are filled with accounts of "Fan Death" (Rebecca Rosen, "The Attack of the Killer Fans," *The Atlantic*, May 2012), where people shut the doors and window of a room, turn on a fan, and die. In the Czech Republic, people avoid the wind from air conditioners and refrigerators for fear of *nastydnout od ledvin* or "catching a cold from the kidneys," which causes "sore trapezoid muscles, headaches, back pain and even rheumatism" (www.jenprozeny.cz/zdravi/20172-co-vam-lete-hrozi-aute). Wind, it seems, carries our fears about the world into our bodies.

199. Wen-Shing Tseng, "The Development of Psychiatric Concepts in Traditional Chinese Medicine," *Archives of General Psychiatry*, October 1973, vol. 29, p. 571.

200. Donald Brown, *Human Universals* (McGraw-Hill Humanities, 1991). Also cited in Steven Pinker's *The Blank Slate: The Modern Denial of Human Nature* (New York: Penguin Books, 2002), p. 437.

201. From the author's interviews with Andrew Gordon.

202. Andrew S. Gordon, Cosmin Adrian Bejan, and Kenji Sagae, "Commonsense Causal Reasoning Using Millions of Personal Stories," *Association for the Advancement of Artificial Intelligence*, 2011.

203. Yuval Noah Hariri, *Sapiens: A Brief History of Humankind* (New York: Harper, 2015), pp. 20–39.

204. See Rutu Mulkar-Mehta, Andrew S. Gordon, Jerry Hobbs, and Eduard Hovy, "Causal Markers Across Domains and Genres of Discourse," K-CAP'11, June 26–29, 2011; and Emmett Tomai, Laxman Thapa, Andrew S. Gordon, and Sin-Hwa Kang, "Causality in Hundreds of Narratives of the Same Events," 2011, Association for the Advancement of Artificial Intelligence.

205. This may happen with the publication of Andrew Gordon's book, *How People Think They Think: A Formal Theory of Commonsense Psychology* (with Jerry Hobbs), a sort of dictionary of causal reasoning (which he calls "a logical formalization of commonsense

knowledge that people have about their own mental lives") that represents more than fifteen years of work on this problem, and could send computers hurling into our lives, and our stories, in a way they never have been before.

206. Eileen Gavin, "The Causal Issue in Empirical Psychology from Hume to the Present, with Emphasis upon the Work of Michotte," *Journal of the History of the Behavioral Sciences*, 1972, vol. 8, no. 3, p. 303.

207. Gavin, 1972, p. 310. See also Albert Michotte, *The Perception of Causality* (New York: Basic Books, 1963). That ability has since been found in infants as young as six months (Lisa Oakes and Leslie Cohen, "Infant Perception of a Causal Event," *Cognitive Development*, 5, 1990, pp. 193–207).

208. Ibid., p. 311.

209. Cited in Daniel Kahneman, *Thinking Fast and Slow* (New York: Farrar, Straus and Giroux, 2011), p. 76. Andrew Gordon has also done work with the Heider-Simmel film. His laboratory has created the Heider-Simmel Interactive Theater, where you can create your own Heider-Simmel film. (narrative.ict.usc.edu/heider-simmel-interactive-theater.html).

210. Camus wrote, "At that subtle moment when man glances backward over his life, Sisyphus returning toward his rock, in that slight pivoting he contemplates that series of unrelated actions which becomes his fate, created by him, combined under his memory's eye and soon sealed by death." While true in some sense, this conjecture is absurd because no one actually does this. We do not see our lives as a series of unrelated events. Humans, by our nature, look back and impose causal coherence on our life events. Without it, all we have is chaos, absurdity and dry philosophical novels. (It's possible Camus suffered from "depressive realism") (Albert Camus, *The Myth of Sisyphus and Other Essays* [New York: Vintage International, 1983], p. 123).

211. Gazzaniga, 2011, p. 85.

212. Ibid., p. 83.

213. Dan McAdams, "The Psychology of Life Stories," *Review of General Psychology*, 2001, vol. 5, no. 2, pp. 100–22.

214. Dan McAdams, *The Redemptive Self: Stories Americans Live By* (Oxford: Oxford University Press, 2006), p. 87.

215. In his book *Creativity: The Psychology of Discovery and Invention*, psychologist Mihaly Csikszentmihalyi tells the story of an artist who, the first time he was interviewed, was young and successful and described his childhood as "perfectly normal, even idyllic." Ten years later when his paintings were no longer in vogue, and his career was in decline, he told Csikszentmihalyi: "His father had been aloof and punishing, his mother pushy and obsessive." Previously he'd talked about his summer days in the orchard. Now he talked about his bedwetting problems. Csikszentmihalyi interviewed him again ten years later, when he was a washed up, twice-divorced alcoholic with a drug problem. "Now," Csikszentmihalyi writes, "his description of childhood included alcoholic fathers and uncles, physical abuse, and emotional tyranny. No wonder the child had failed as an adult. Which version of his early years was closer to the truth?" There is, Csikszentmihalyi observes, "a powerful pressure to make the past consistent with the present," which is another way of saying we look for, and find, causal cohesion in our lives (Csikszentmihalyi, *Creativity: The Flow and Psychology of Discovery and Invention* [New York: HarperPerennial, 1996], pp. 172–73). The stories we tell about the world, too, are often indicative of our inner state than of anything outside us. In a study at the University of Buffalo, 395 adults were asked to write about the September 11, 2001, terrorist attacks. Then, their stories were compared to results on a test of their psychological well-being. It turned out people with better mental health told different kinds of stories that those with poorer health. The first group's stories were, "high in closure, high in redemptive imagery and high in themes of national redemption." The latter's were "low

in closure, high in contaminative imagery and high in themes of personal contamination" (Jonathan Adler et al., "The Political Is Personal: Narrating 9/11 and Psychological Well-Being," *Journal of Personality*, August 2009, 77 [4], pp. 903–32).

216. James Pennebaker, *Opening Up: The Healing Power of Expressing Emotions* (New York: The Guildford Press, 1997), p. 6.

217. Ibid., p. 30.

218. Ibid., p. 34.

219. Ibid., pp. 36–37.

220. Another of Pennebaker's studies looked at employees who'd been laid off from a large computer company in Dallas with no warning. They averaged fifty-two years old. Most had worked for the company for thirty years. The men were divided into three groups. One wrote about "their deepest thoughts and feelings about getting laid off" for thirty minutes a day over five days. Another group wrote about time management. A third group wrote about nothing at all. Within three months, 27 percent of the first group had jobs, compared to 5 percent of the other groups. After several months, 53 percent of the first group had jobs, compared to 18 percent of the others. They all went to exactly the same number of job interviews (Pennebaker 1997, pp. 38–40).

221. Kelli Keough and Hazel Markus, "The Role of the Self in Building the Bridge from Philosophy to Biology," *Psychological Inquiry*, 1998, 9, pp. 49–53. Cited in McGonigal, 2015, p. 70.

222. Two important studies along these lines, cited in Moerman, 2002, pp. 89–93: L. Luborsky, B. Singer, et al., "Comparative Studies of Psychotherapies. Is It True That 'Everyone Has Won and All Must Have Prizes'?" *Archives of General Psychiatry*, 1975, 32, pp. 995–1008. And M. L. Smith and G. V. Glass, "Meta-analysis of Psychotherapy Outcome Studies," *American Psychologist*, 1977, 32, pp. 752–60.

223. In a study of Sudanese refugees, subjects were given four sessions of Narrative Exposure Therapy (NET), supportive counseling, or

"psychoeducation." A year later, only 29 percent of the NET group still fulfilled PTSD criteria, while 79 percent and 80 percent of the other groups did, respectively (Frank Neuner, Margarete Schauer, et al., "A Comparison of Narrative Exposure Therapy, Supportive Counseling, and Psychoeducation for Treating Posttraumatic Stress Disorder in an African Refugee Settlement," *Journal of Consulting and Clinical Psychology* 2004, vol. 72, no. 4, pp. 579–87). In another study, twenty-six Rwandan genocide orphans were divided into two groups. One was given NET. The other was given interpersonal psychotherapy. At six months, 25 percent of the NET children still fulfilled the PTSD criteria, while 71 percent of the therapy group did. The NET group was also much improved on depression compared to the second (Susanne Schaal, Thomas Elbert, and Frank Neuner, "Narrative Exposure Therapy Versus Group Interpersonal Psychotherapy: A Controlled Clinical Trial with Orphaned Survivors of the Rwandan Genocide," *Psychotherapy and Psychosomatics*, 2009, 78, pp. 298–306).

224. Maggie Schauer, Frank Neuner, and Thomas Elbert, *Narrative Exposure Therapy: A Short-Term Treatment For Traumatic Stress Disorders*, 2nd edition (Cambridge, MA: Hogrefe Publishing, 2011).

225. Lamaro P. Onyut, Frank Neuner, et al., "Narrative Exposure Therapy as a Treatment for Child War Survivors with Posttraumatic Stress Disorder: Two Case Reports and a Pilot Study in an African Refugee Settlement," *Biomed Central Psychiatry*, 2005, 5:7.

Chapter 12: The Worm Turns

226. Jilek, 1986, p. 279.

Chapter 13: Beyond Belief

227. All three examples from Sunanda Creagh, "Mass Trance Afflicts Indonesian Factory Workers," Reuters/Yahoo News, February 24, 2008.

228. John Croman, "Minnesota School Incident Likely Mass Psychogenic Illness," KARE 11 News, February 8, 2014.

229. Laura Dimon, "What Witchcraft Is Facebook? Mass Psychogenic Illness—Historically Known as 'Mass Hysteria'—Is Making a Comeback," *The Atlantic*, September 11, 2013.

230. Robert Bartholomew et al., "Mass Psychogenic Illness and the Social Network: Is It Changing the Pattern of Outbreaks?" *Journal of the Royal Society Medical of Medicine*, 2012, 105, pp. 509–12. See also Susan Dominus, "What Happened to the Girls in Le Roy?" *New York Times Magazine*, March 7, 2012.

231. Heiner Raspe, Angelika Hueppe, and Hannelore Neuhauser, "Back Pain, a Communicable Disease?" International Journal of Epidemiology, 2008, 37, p. 72.

232. Ibid. For more, see Raspe, et al., 2008, pp. 69–74.

233. Nicholas Christakis and James Fowler, "The Spread of Obesity in a Large Social Network over 32 Years," *The New England Journal of Medicine*, 2007, 357, pp. 370–79. See also Nicholas Christakis, and James Fowler, *Connected: The Surprising Power of Our Social Networks and How They Shape Our Lives* (New York: Little, Brown and Company, 2009).

234. Nicholas Christakis and James Fowler, "The Collective Dynamics of Smoking in a Large Social Network," *New England Journal of Medicine* 2008, 358: 2249–58.

235. Rose McDermott, James H. Fowler, and Nicholas A. Christakis, "Breaking Up Is Hard to Do, Unless Everyone Else Is Doing It Too: Social Network Effects on Divorce in a Longitudinal Sample," *Social Science Research Network*, October 18, 2009. See also "Is Divorce Contagious?" Pew Research Center, October 21, 2013: www.pewresearch.org/fact-tank/2013/10/21/is-divorce-contagious/.

236. Christakis and Fowler found that the spread of happiness flows socially, but *is* also dependent on geography: When you have a friend who lives within a mile who becomes happy, your chance

of becoming happy increases by 25 percent. If a sibling who lives within a mile becomes happy, the probability of that happiness passing to you is 14 percent. The effect lasts about a year. If the connection lives more than a mile away, there is no effect (Christakis and Fowler, *Connected*, 2009, pp. 49–54).

237. John Cacioppo, an expert in the science of loneliness, partnered with Christakis and Fowler and found that if a person had a friend or family member who was lonely, there was 52 percent chance he or she would be lonely two years later (Christakis and Fowler, *Connected*, 2009, pp. 57–59. Also: John T. Cacioppo, James Fowler, and Nicholas Christakis, "Alone in the Crowd: The Structure and Spread of Loneliness in a Large Social Network," *Journal of Personality and Social Psychology*, December 2009; 97[6]: pp. 977–91).

238. A study of "cognitive style" among college roommates found that after three months, students with a positive or negative attitude began to adopt each other's attitude. And just six months of living with a roommate with a negative attitude significantly increased the risk of depression (Gerald J. Haeffel and Jennifer L. Hames, "Cognitive Vulnerability to Depression Can Be Contagious," *Clinical Psychological Science* April 16, 2013, cited on NPR, "Gloomy Thinking Can Be Contagious," June 24, 2013: www.npr.org /sections/health-shots/2013/06/24/193483931/Contagious-Thinking-Can-Be-Depressing). Kindness too can spread socially (James Fowler and Nicholas Christakis, "Cooperative Behavior Cascades in Human Social Networks," *PNAS*, March 23, 2010, vol. 107, no. 12, pp. 5334–38.

239. According to the Cultural Niche theory of evolution, social learning is at the core of humankind's rapid rise. It's how we accumulate knowledge over generations and is what separates us from other primates. We have the ability to pass on causal perception without causal knowledge. We can know one thing causes another to happen without knowing how it does. (Do you know how your computer

works? Your car?) This is called "abductive reasoning" and it is our strength as a species (as well as—sometimes—our weakness). Social learning is the most powerful transmitter of casual perception and plays a major role in everything from Robin Dunbar's social brain theory to the placebo effect to the interpersonal health effect. (Robert Boyd, Peter J. Richerson, and Joseph Henrich, "The Cultural Niche: Why Social Learning Is Essential for Human Adaptation," *PNAS*, June 28, 2011, vol. 108, no. Supplement 2, pp. 10918–25. See also Joseph Henrich, "A Cultural Species: How Culture Drove Human Evolution; A Multi-Disciplinary Framework for Understanding Culture, Cognition and Behavior," *Psychological Science Agenda* [American Psychological Association], November 2011.)

240. Luana Colloca and Fabrizio Benedetti, "Placebo Analgesia Induced by Social Observational Learning," *Pain*, 2009, pp. 28–34; and Fabrizio Benedetti, "Responding to Nocebos Through Observation: Social Contagion of Negative Emotions," *Pain*, 2013, 154, p. 1165.

241. In a study of 10,000 school students, Catherine Riegle-Crumb investigated the gender gap in girls studying physics, and found that the gap had nothing to do with income, or inner city vs. suburbs or any other typical cause. The only factor that mattered was having more women in the community working in science, technology, engineering, and math. In those communities, girls were just as likely to study physics as boys. They saw a scientific life being lived around them and knew it was a path they could follow (Catherine Riegle-Crumb and Chelsea Moore, "The Gender Gap in High School Physics: Considering the Context of Local Communities," *Social Science Quarterly*, March 2014, vol. 95, iss. 1, pp. 253–68. Cited on Shankar Vedantam, "Why Aren't More Girls Attracted to Physics?" August 9, 2013: www.npr.org/templates /transcript/transcript.php?storyId=210251404.

242. To put a finer point on this, what I mean is that when we use the word "culture" we're talking about the ecosystem of stories we feel

we are part of and that we share with a group of people, either by birth or by choice. By "stories" I mean the full spectrum of causal chains, from the shortest (how to interact with people you meet) to the longest (how the universe came into being). I mean stories about the past, the present, and the future. I mean stories about heroes and villains and ordinary people getting through their lives. I mean stories about the physical and spiritual worlds, stories about luck and love and loss. Because in each story there is some causal force that feels at first possible, then familiar, then real. These causal perceptions—these beliefs—are the missing piece of the bioloop.

243. Bill Gardner, "Author Paul Gruchow, Who Chronicled the Prairie, Dies at 56," *St. Paul Pioneer Press*, February 24, 2004.

244. Mike Finley, "Empty Places: Remembering Paul Gruchow," *Minnesota Monthly*, November 2004.

Chapter 14: To the Sea

245. The Li language spoken in Shuiman is closer to Thai than to Mandarin or Cantonese, and the villagers don't look anything like people in Beijing. Even in the 1980s, the Li and Miao (Hmong) tribes had their own autonomous government in Wuzhishan. That ended around the same time the first roads connected Shuiman to the outside world. Now you can get there on a bike.

246. Schafer, 1970, p. 27.

247. "Hainan, a Mother Because of 'Witches' Were Burnt to Death Called Yaoqi Three Sons," *South China Sea Network*, Kunming Harbor, August 8, 2012: news.kunming.cn/society/content/2012-08/22/content_3056274.htm. (Title as rendered by Google Translate.)

INDEX

About the Author

FRANK BURES's stories have appeared in *Harper's Maga-zine, Outside, Esquire, Bicycling, Men's Health, Scientific American Mind*, and *The Washington Post Magazine*, and have been included in a number of *Best American Travel Writing* anthologies. He has lived in several countries and currently resides in Minneapolis.